Pathways to Intimacy

Dr. Michael Don Howard

Conversations For Closeness - Creating The Marriage You Have Always Dreamed Of

ISBN: 1463598327
ISBN-13: 9781463598327

Introduction

Marriage is a relationship unlike any other. If all goes well we will live with our spouse longer than we will live with any other person in our entire life. With a divorce rate in the United States of over 50% however, one can only wonder what the likelihood of success might actually be. There are many things that contribute to problematic marriages. Couples are inundated with a variety of daily and transitional stressors that create significant hardships, challenges, and conflict. When we marry, we have dreams of love, excitement, and a future built upon a framework of intimacy, affection, passion, common interests, and mutual care and respect. We seek to marry the person we believe to be our best friend. We begin the marriage in what many refer to as the honeymoon phase only to soon discover the realities of marriage...the good, bad, and ugly. For some, this reality sadly consists of much more bad than good. For the rest, marriage is a great and joyous thing, with dramatically more good than bad. This is what I want for all of us...and the good news is that it is possible. This book has been written to help you get there – to achieve the marriage you dream of.

Many books have been written on the subject of marriages and building good relationships. This book will hopefully be more than just another self-help relationship book. Instead, I hope to give you, the reader, a new experience - an opportunity to approach your marriage from a different perspective. Through personal experience with my own marriage of more than 25 years and working with numerous couples as a Licensed Marriage and Family Therapist and as a Chaplain in the United States Navy, I have concluded that the key to forming, building, and maintaining a successful love-filled marriage is the creation of intimacy. That will be the framework from which this book approaches the complex topic of marriage.

As you read, ponder, and apply the words contained on the following pages it is my hope and prayer that your marriage will grow into the one you dreamed of when you said "I do." There are seven chapters in this book. Each has been written for a distinct purpose and each is critically important in its own unique way. Each chapter has been intentionally made relatively short so that you and your spouse do not become overwhelmed, bored, or tired of simply reading and digesting the written material. What makes this book different in my opinion is what takes place at the end of the chapter. I am referring to an opportunity for you and your spouse to create a level of intimacy in your marriage like you have never seen or experienced before.

At the end of each chapter are a series of detailed, thought-provoking questions pertaining to the subject of that particular chapter. This is the most important part of the book. Take your time individually to answer these questions as thoroughly and thoughtfully as you possibly can. Be specific in your responses and do not share your responses with your spouse at this point. Once you are both finished, come together and in a setting free of distractions, share your responses to the questions and have a meaningful and loving discussion about those responses. Take the time to really understand each other. Take the time to see why he or she feels the way that they do. Take the time to express your thoughts, opinions, and beliefs in a way that is respectful and loving. This process will bring you closer than ever. It will also help you create the marriage you have dreamed of.

Best wishes for a life of happiness, joy, and intimacy.

Dedication

This book is the culmination of efforts over a period of several years. It would not be possible without the love and support of my beautiful and loving wife, Lonna; as well as our amazing children: Ila, Dawn, Kimberly, and Jonathan. All of you have inspired and motivated me in unique ways. I also want to thank the Sailors, Marines, and military families that I have had the privilege to work with over the last 27 years. You give my life purpose and you are the reason for this book. God Bless America! Finally, and most importantly, I wish to thank my Heavenly Father. This book would not be possible without His love, grace, and mercy. He has strengthened me and inspired me. It is my prayer that this book will bring glory to God.

Table of Contents

CHAPTER ONE

Family Roles & Responsibilities

With more women entering the workforce and couples feeling the need to maintain two incomes to survive or get ahead financially, the decision of who does what around the home is a monumental one. Many of us grew up in more traditional homes where the labor boundaries were considered pretty cut and dry. Husbands were typically the breadwinners or the ones responsible for earning a living and subsequently providing for the financial security and physical needs of the family. Many husbands were also the ones to take care of the vehicles, fix things around the house, and even care for the yard. Wives traditionally maintained the inside of the house and cared for the children and the daily needs of the family. This included the demanding tasks of driving children to and from activities, helping with homework, as well as doing the cooking, cleaning, and washing of clothes. This is not necessarily the case today. Some might echo the sentiments of the popular movie "we're not in Kansas anymore." I grew up in a traditional household very similar to the one described above. This experience impacted my belief system and directly affected my expectations of household roles and what marriage should be like. I have done a poor job of supporting my wife around the house, but fortunately for me, she has adapted to my selfishness and/or laziness, and puts up with me despite my imperfections.

As I previously stated, the typical family of today is quite different. The wife is more likely to work outside the home. She is more likely to have a college education and a career that provides income, opportunity, and self-fulfillment. This can however, create significant challenges for the couple. The question of priorities, roles and responsibilities, and management of time and other resources all become important considerations. The first issue requiring some attention is the question of why the wife might decide to work outside the home in the first place and what factors contribute to this decision. This decision, as well as its subsequent impact on the family system, is particularly complex and difficult if the couple has children at home.

Some women work outside the home because the couple believes they need the additional income. It is great to have more money coming in each month and having a second income can provide enormous financial stability and added security. The problem with this logic however, is that it precludes us from looking at the larger cost/benefit picture and we are lulled into the mental trap of believing that we must have that second income because we need it. We begin to believe that we would never be able to function without it. Perhaps the greatest obstacle to achieving financial security for individuals, couples, and families alike is the inability to distinguish needs from wants. Couples must assess whether they need or want the additional income and if they subsequently decide that both of them will work outside the home, what will be the associated cost of this decision? Many couples are surprised to find that it can actually cost more in the long-run for the spouse to work – especially once child care costs and additional taxes are factored in.

On the other hand, in addition to the potential financial benefits of working outside the home, there may be a host of personal ones as well. Individuals want the satisfaction that comes from feeling as though they are making a difference. They also want the friendships and professional relationships that are formed in the work place. They may feel unfulfilled or dissatisfied at home, feeling that they want or deserve more than a life that requires them to be home all day caring for a husband, children, and the household. Working outside the home can also have a significant positive impact on the self-esteem of the wife in many cases. I believe that it is easy for women to feel as though they are caught in the middle of wanting to be at home with their children, while at the same time wanting to have a successful and meaningful career outside the home. This is a difficult position to be in and I don't envy women for this. This tension can lead to a host of negative feelings, potentially resulting in problems individually and in relationships with others. Many of these problems are discussed later in this chapter and throughout the remainder of this book.

Along with the numerous advantages that working outside the home offers women, there are also many disadvantages. It is extremely difficult for women to balance the demands of home, work, and family. I have had several frustrated wives tell me about working all day only to come home and cook, clean, and take care of the children prior to going to bed. They then have to get up the next morning and begin the whole process over again. Mothers sometimes report feeling conflicted because they know they deserve the same opportunities for professional success that men have, but many also feel that they have a responsibility at home and should be doing more for or with their children and family. They oftentimes feel guilty, falling prey to the misguided belief that working outside the home is a selfish act. This internal struggle can result in feelings of guilt that they may subsequently have difficulty forgiving themselves for. They may even feel that they are choosing money and career over their own children.

When women work outside the home there may be some significant negative feelings directed towards the husband. This is especially true if the wife feels that she has been forced to work. She may resent her husband for not making enough money, not working hard enough, or not being able to budget and manage the household finances. This may add to the dynamic mentioned earlier, feeling they are forced to choose work over being a mother. The difference in this particular situation however, is that they blame the husband for the choice or perceived lack thereof. These feelings will potentially serve as a barrier between the couple – a wall composed of bitterness, resentment, and/or anger.

Another dynamic I have seen in couples where only the husband works outside the home is that he can feel overwhelming pressure to support the family financially and may even come to resent or harbor ill-feelings towards his wife for not bringing home a paycheck. This is especially true if he feels that the extra income would give them things they currently can't afford. Resentment will potentially be even higher if the husband feels that his wife is doing an inadequate job in her responsibilities at home. A lot of this hinges most directly on his expectations of her and whether or not she is living up to them. In his mind, she is staying home and they are sacrificing additional income so that she can do a job that he perceives as being poorly accomplished. This leaves him most likely feeling unsupported and alone in his efforts to lead the family.

When deciding whether or not both you and your spouse should work outside the home, it may be useful to consider the following questions and then engage in a thoughtful and respectful conversation in which you discuss the needs, hopes, and dreams surrounding this very important issue as they pertain to you both as individuals and together as a couple. The first question you, as a couple, must ask yourselves is a financial one. "Do you make enough money with one income to pay all of your bills and to support yourself and your family?" If the answer to this question is yes then a second income is likely not necessary, at least not from a financial perspective. This question forces you, as a couple, to address the issue of needs vs. wants. The problem is that it is so easy to become accustomed to the extra money and the material things that a second income provides. This is precisely why it is difficult for individuals, couples, and families to give up a second income. Additional income starts off as something extra and quickly becomes a required and much necessary part of the budget.

The next question you must ask yourself is "assuming you do need a second income, are there things you can give up or ways that you can cut back in an effort to reduce your bills, debts, and expenditures enough so that you do not need to rely on a second income?" For example, are there possessions that you can sell? Are there things that you can minimize or eliminate from your monthly budget? If so, a second income is probably not necessary, from a purely financial perspective at least. This might be good time to have a yard sell or cancel the premium cable programs.

The next financially related question you, as a couple must ask yourselves is whether you need the second income to save for the purchase of a specific item. For example, you may want a second income to save for a new vehicle, home, vacation, special gift, or college education. Again, the question of needs vs. wants comes into play and the couple must address that issue as well as whether or not there are other ways to save the money. For example, you may find other ways (e.g., investments or short-term work projects) to slowly save for a new car, thus preventing yourself from feeling as though you need two incomes to make ends meet.

Finally, you, as the wife, must address the question of whether you simply want or feel the need to work outside the home. There are many women who want to work outside the home and feel as though they have as much right as men to do so. I have had women tell me that they can't cope with the stress of being at home, taking care of children all day. They feel they must work in order to maintain their emotional health. In cases such as this, the question of whether the wife will work is not only a financial one, but a physical, emotional, and even spiritual one as well. It is worth noting that there are times where the question of concern is not whether or not one spouse should stay home, but rather, which one should. I have met many couples where either the income potential of the wife is higher than the husband, or the husband simply prefers to stay home while the wife prefers to be out in the work force. This may seem unconventional, but it works well for some and poorly for others.

Couples facing the question of whether or not they should both work outside the home should sit down together and have a very intentional and proactive conversation about this extremely important issue (see the exercise at the end of the chapter for more detail on how to accomplish this task). They must come prepared to address both the financial and psychological aspects of the decision as well.

They must examine their family histories, beliefs, and values concerning mothers working outside the home. They must also be honest with themselves and with each other about their feelings and perceived needs regarding working outside the home. They must communicate their needs regarding this issue to their spouse. For example, a wife who wants to work for her own self-fulfillment must tell her husband that she wants to work because it makes her feel important; that what she does matters, and that by working outside the home, she is contributing to the workforce and community in which they live. A husband might say to his wife that he wants her to work so that they can afford to take trips together periodically; hoping that this will help them maintain a more satisfying and loving marital relationship. A wife might also say to her husband that motherhood is important and that to her, nothing is more significant than being there for her children and that because of these beliefs, she wants to be a stay-at-home mom. She subsequently tells him that she needs him to support her in this extremely important role.

Assuming the couple reaches the decision that both of them should work, they must then negotiate roles and responsibilities within the home. This same issue applies to all couples, but is more critical and challenging for dual-income couples. Many couples have an extremely difficult time negotiating household responsibilities. As husband and wife, we tend to act in ways that resemble the patterns shown to us by our parents within our family of origin. A husband will more likely help with the housework, cooking, cleaning, and tending to the children if his father did these types of things. Similarly, wives will do more of the mechanical tasks around the house, help out in the yard, and complete minor car repairs if those are things that her mother routinely did. In other words, we develop our expectations of what we and our spouses will do around the house in part from what we saw our own parents doing.

An extremely important aspect of the modeling behavior of our parents and others that we observed as children is that it helps to form our expectations of what we expect from our spouse. Imagine if you will, the following scenario: A husband (Tom) and wife (Susan) have just had their first baby. Both work outside the home, but Susan is becoming increasingly frustrated and angry at Tom because she feels that she has to do all of the work and that he is unwilling to help out around the house. As a child, Susan remembers her father and mother sharing responsibilities within the home. Her father would cook dinner at least 2-3 times a week, do some light cleaning and other household chores at night and on the weekends when time permitted, and would even help with the children much of the time. Tom's parents were quite different. His mother was a stay-at-home mom and did everything to care for the house, her husband, and the children. Tom's father worked long hours, spent much of his time on weekends doing yard work, but rarely, if ever, helped out inside the home. It would make sense, taking into consideration these previous experiences, Tom would expect that Susan would take care of the home and the children (even if she did work outside the home) and Susan would expect that she and Tom would share much of the workload. This dilemma escalated with time and became the source of major marital conflict for this young couple.

Just as before, Tom and Susan must first decide whether Susan will work outside the home. This decision however, leads to further questions regarding how they will divide and share the responsibilities around the house. They probably don't really know or understand how different their family backgrounds are and to what extent these early experiences have influenced their expectations regarding roles and responsibilities within the marriage and around the house. This lack of understanding will make it increasingly difficult for Tom and Susan to be able to communicate and eventually solve this important problem. If unable to resolve the issue, Susan will likely continue to feel unsupported, lonely, and resentful. She will communicate these feelings to Tom directly through snide comments and angry outbursts and passively through a variety of nonverbal behaviors. Tom will have difficulty responding to Susan in an effective and meaningful way and will either respond with anger, causing the interaction between them to escalate, or he will withdraw emotionally and/or physically. Either reaction will be problematic and result in further contention between them.

So by now you are asking yourselves what you can do if you are in a situation like that of Tom and Susan. Begin by realizing that this is not a small or insignificant issue and that it is important that you sit down together as a couple and discuss these things patiently, honestly, and openly. Examine your family of origin and ask yourself what you observed and learned with regards to how husbands and wives share responsibilities and what roles each have. Once you have both taken some time to do this, honestly evaluate how you personally share responsibility with your spouse around the house and in what areas you or your spouse might like to make changes. Once this is complete, sit down together with your spouse and openly discuss what you have learned regarding your family of origin and how you currently share household responsibility with your spouse. Ask your spouse for his or her input, insight, and feelings regarding this exchange of information and his or her reaction to it. This is an important issue to discuss, but even more importantly, it is a wonderful opportunity to connect in an emotional, heartfelt, and caring manner. These conversations will bring you closer together as a couple and will help you find a better way to work together as a couple. It will also help you to more fully appreciate one another and to share that appreciation with your spouse.

FAMILY ROLES & RESPONSIBILITIES

Couple Exercise

Instructions: Answer the following questions as completely and honestly as possible. Do not share your answers with your spouse until both of you have finished answering these questions.

1. Describe your family of origin with regards to the role your mother or other female caregiver(s) took in working outside the home.

_____

_____

_____

_____

_____

_____

_____

_____

_____

_____

_____

_____

_____

_____

_____

_____

_____

_____

_____

_____

_____

_____

_____

_____

_____

_____

2. What are your personal beliefs about women working outside the home? Does your view change if there are children in the home? Y / N If so, in what ways?

_____

_____

_____

_____

_____

_____

_____

_____

_____

_____

_____

_____

_____

_____

_____

_____

_____

_____

_____

_____

_____

_____

_____

_____

_____

_____

_____

_____

_____

_____

_____

_____

_____

_____

_____

3. What do you believe your spouse's views on women working outside the home to be?

_____

_____

_____

_____

_____

_____

_____

_____

_____

_____

_____

_____

_____

_____

_____

_____

_____

_____

_____

_____

_____

_____

_____

_____

_____

_____

_____

_____

_____

_____

_____

_____

_____

_____

_____

_____

_____

4. Do you (or does your wife) want to work outside the home? Y / N Why or why not?

_____
_____
_____
_____
_____
_____
_____
_____
_____
_____
_____
_____
_____
_____
_____
_____
_____
_____
_____
_____
_____
_____
_____
_____
_____
_____
_____
_____
_____
_____
_____
_____
_____

5. Do you feel that you financially need a second income? Why or why not?

_____

_____

_____

_____

_____

_____

_____

_____

_____

_____

_____

_____

_____

_____

_____

_____

_____

_____

_____

_____

_____

_____

_____

_____

_____

_____

_____

_____

_____

_____

_____

_____

_____

_____

_____

_____

_____

_____

6. If you feel that you need a second income, can you eliminate that need by reducing your debt or spending? Y / N If so, how? If not, Why?

_____

_____

_____

_____

_____

_____

_____

_____

_____

_____

_____

_____

_____

_____

_____

_____

_____

_____

_____

_____

_____

_____

_____

_____

_____

_____

_____

_____

_____

_____

_____

_____

_____

7. What does your spouse (husband or wife) working outside the home mean to the marriage and to you as a partner in the marriage?

_____

_____

_____

_____

_____

_____

_____

_____

_____

_____

_____

_____

_____

_____

_____

_____

_____

_____

_____

_____

_____

_____

_____

_____

_____

_____

_____

_____

_____

_____

_____

_____

_____

_____

_____

8. How are the specific family roles and responsibilities divided around the house currently? What do you like and/or dislike about this arrangement?

_____
_____
_____
_____
_____
_____
_____
_____
_____
_____
_____
_____
_____
_____
_____
_____
_____
_____
_____
_____
_____
_____
_____
_____
_____
_____
_____
_____
_____
_____
_____
_____
_____
_____
_____
_____

9. What would your spouse say you do around the house to help out?

_____

_____

_____

_____

_____

_____

_____

_____

_____

_____

_____

_____

_____

_____

_____

_____

_____

_____

_____

_____

_____

_____

_____

_____

_____

_____

_____

_____

_____

_____

_____

_____

_____

_____

_____

10. What do you think your spouse would like you to do more of around the house? How do you feel about this? What is keeping you from doing these things and why?

_____

_____

_____

_____

_____

_____

_____

_____

_____

_____

_____

_____

_____

_____

_____

_____

_____

_____

_____

_____

_____

_____

_____

_____

_____

_____

_____

_____

_____

_____

_____

_____

_____

_____

_____

_____

Now that you have answered these questions, sit down with your spouse and discuss each of these questions and how you answered them. Pay particular attention to needs, feelings, and messages that are developed through the discussion.

<u>Action Plan</u>: As a couple, we have decided to make the following changes or to start doing the following things with regards to family roles and responsibilities: We will sit down and discuss our progress on this plan in 4 weeks.

(Date and time of next meeting) _____

_____

_____

_____

_____

_____

_____

_____

_____

_____

_____

_____

_____

_____

_____

_____

_____

_____

_____

_____

_____

_____

_____

_____

_____

_____

_____

_____

_____

_____

_____

_____

_____

_____

CHAPTER TWO

Finances

Finances are one of the biggest stressors impacting couples today. With the United States facing economic recession and unemployment figures at almost record highs, couples are oftentimes doing all they can just to hold their heads above water. That being said however, many couples are simply doing it to themselves – causing their own pain and suffering. Mismanagement of family finances is one of the leading issues negatively impacting couples and for many, has become a major source of contention and a big reason why they fight, argue, and even divorce. It doesn't have to be this way however. If bad financial habits are replaced with good ones, couples can learn how to manage their finances in a manner that promotes financial health and prosperity, facilitates a life of debt-free living, and results in a happier marital relationship.

My wife and I have struggled significantly in the area of financial responsibility and only recently have we got ourselves to the point where we are actually managing our finances with a sense of maturity and personal responsibility. It has not been easy, and although we are not completely there yet, things are so much better than they used to be. One of the most interesting aspects of this journey towards financial health is that it has caused us to think about and respond to financial situations differently. In other words, it has changed the way we actually think about money and wealth.

In this chapter, as we go through some of the realities of financial management from a couple perspective, I will attempt to share with you some very practical tools that have either worked for my wife and I or that I know for certain have worked for other couples. Realize however, I am not wealthy, and I am not an investment counselor. I have recently become a Certified Financial Coach with Crown Financial Ministries and I am a Licensed Marriage and Family Therapist, but most of what I learned about financial management I learned by first doing it wrong and literally screwing things up. It is my hope and prayer that my words here will save you the pain and heartache that I have experienced because of money. What is particularly nice about financial responsibility is that it leads to acceptance, gratitude, and contentment. For my wife and I it has also led to less arguing about silly matters of money that have little to nothing to do with real happiness. Understand what I am saying here: money and wealth will never equal happiness. It used to be that I would go home, see bills on the table or open one of those dreaded letters from the bank saying that we bounced a check and it was "game on." My attitude and emotional state would transform itself from happy and pleasant to one of disgust within seconds. The evening was essentially over at that point as anger, tension, blame, and resentment flooded the house. Now I go home, bills are paid, there are no letters from the bank, and we are able to relax, spend time together and spend time doing what couples should be doing - loving one another. We have to watch our spending, but we do so in a proactive and responsible way as opposed to a reactive one. The bottom line is that life (and our marriage) is much better and if we can do it….so can you.

I have a brother who is an economist and although he could probably speak much more intelligently than I can on the topic of finances, I want to talk to you from the perspective of the couple…and show you how to rid your relationship of financial stress forever. As I have already stated, this is a critical issue, one that causes couples incredible and unnecessary stress. It is not about wealth, money, or material possessions; but rather, is about how we manage what we do have and out attitudes about it. These attitudes come from many sources – our families growing up, friends and colleagues, media, and society to name a few. Society teaches us that "the person with the most toys wins." The media equates wealth with success and power. Celebrities show us that beauty can be bought. With all of these distorted messages, it is no wonder that we are messed up when it comes to money and wealth.

We will begin our discussion by focusing on the practical aspects of family finances and financial management and then we will focus on the more abstract ideas and concepts related to thoughts, feelings, and attitudes about money, wealth, and how we, as couples, interact on this vital issue. You would probably agree with the idea that most people wish they had more money. We dream of owning that expensive house or brand new car, and we fantasize about winning the lottery or striking it rich in Vegas. Countless people have tried the latest in get-rich schemes, have bought stock in the newest high-tech startup company, or have listened to a friend or other family member regarding the best way to make money fast.

The reality is that most people to not become rich overnight. In fact, most people do not become rich at all. Wealth is an elusive dream that many spend their entire life working and searching for, but only a very few find it. The very few wealthy people that I personally know have told me that it did not happen by winning the lottery, gaining a large inheritance, or developing some magical or revolutionary product. Instead, they say that it came through sacrifice, making good financial decisions, and most importantly, staying out of debt. This last point is critically important as it relates to the statement, "Why pay someone else when you could pay yourself instead?" Looking at it another way, it would be wiser and more beneficial to earn interest on savings and investments as opposed to paying interest on something that is depreciating in value by the minute. Compound interest is one of the miracles of life and is one of the key elements of true financial success.

Eliminating debt is the number one secret to becoming wealthy or gaining financial freedom. The problem is that becoming debt free is difficult and can require months and even years of sacrifice and patience. It begins by taking an honest look at your personal finances. You must prepare an accurate monthly budget by looking at your monthly income and comparing that with your expenditures for the same period of time. Using figure (1) at the back of this chapter as an example, enter your monthly income and then enter the amount you spend per month in each of the categories provided. You may need to adjust or change the categories based on your personal situation. For example, if you do not have pets, you can delete the column labeled pet expenses. If you are like many couples, you may not realize how much you actually spend in each of these different areas. Therefore, it is important that you determine these values by tracking your expenses. This may take several months to get accurate values, but the spending plan should be used immediately by utilizing projected values and then adjusting them with time as more accurate data is obtained.

Tracking expenses is a very powerful process because as people monitor their spending, they will be more aware and as a result, will typically spend less. This enables them to have more money left to put towards paying off debt. If all goes according to plan, they can use the extra money to pay off their debt by focusing on one specific debt at a time. This process has been referred to as snowballing or power-paying one's debt. An example of how this is done is shown in figure (2) at the back of this chapter. Assume for example, that a couple has five items of debt. This includes a car, two credit cards, and two consumer credit accounts. Also assume that the car balance is $10,000 with a monthly payment of $350 and an interest rate of 7% with two years remaining on the loan. The credit cards have a balance of $1,400 and $1,500 with interest rates of 13% and 16% respectively. The consumer credit accounts have a balance of $1,100 and $1,000 with interest rates of 17% and 21% respectively. It may surprise you to learn that if a couple makes the minimum monthly payment on a credit card with a $1,000 balance and an 18% interest rate, it will take them approximately eight years to pay it off. Couples often complain of credit card balances actually rising each month due to finance charges and associated fees.

The couple must determine which debt to work towards paying off. Typically, it is best to pay off those with the highest interest rate or highest monthly payment first for obvious financial reasons, but it may actually be best to work toward paying off the debt that has the lowest balance first (even if the interest rate is lower). Paying off the smaller debt first gives the couple a taste of success and will serve to motivate and encourage them to keep working and sacrificing - to stay on the road towards becoming debt free and financially secure. Therefore, in the example given in figure (2), I would recommend paying off the two consumer credit accounts first, then the two credit cards, and finally, the car.

The way this works is that the couple determines how much extra cash can be devoted to paying off debt. The important element here is that there must be a surplus of income (no matter how small) for this to work. The couple will determine how much extra money can be diverted to paying off debt by using the spending plan developed in figure (1). This extra money is allocated to the debt that the couple wants paid off first. While paying the extra money on this one debt, the couple makes the minimum payment on all other debts. Once the first debt is paid off, the couple devotes all of the money going towards that debt to the second debt until it is paid off. Once this happens, all of that money (plus the minimum payment already being made) is devoted towards the third debt. This process continues until the couple finds themselves debt free. It is not uncommon for couples to become debt-free within a fraction of the time they initially thought possible if they are disciplined and stick to the plan. A very important consideration if this plan is to work is for the couple not to add or take on any additional debt. I recommend cutting up all credit cards except one (for things such as booking flights, hotels, and perhaps going out to dinner). There is nothing wrong with having one credit card for convenience if it is completely paid off every month so as to not accrue any interest. If even one card is too much to handle, then I strongly recommend that you cut up all the cards so as to avoid the temptation of over-spending or debting all together.

The problem with paying off credit cards and consumer accounts and then keeping them active is that the person may see the available credit as an opportunity and immediately go back to spending irrationally with little to no discipline. A similar problem occurs when people obtain debt consolidation loans. The money is used to pay off the debt and in return typically has a lower interest rate with a lower overall monthly payment. It may also be easier for the couple to manage their financial records since payments are going to one location as opposed to many different ones. This may sound great on the surface, but as usual, there is more to consider. As Paul Harvey would say, "And now for the rest of the story..." The problem with consolidation loans is that it is extremely easy to charge the accounts right back up to where they were, thus leaving the person worse off than before because they now have a consolidation loan payment on top of maxed out credit cards. Home equity lines of credit are also bad because people see them as an unlimited source of extra money from which they can buy things for the house or make much sought after home improvements. The net result is more money owed to the bank and subsequently, more interest paid in the process. Home refinancing options are also problematic because banks will often convince consumers to borrow higher amounts, up to ninety percent of the home value in some cases. This can leave the person with a higher payment and in the case of a shift in the housing market (such as that experienced in most parts of the country in the last few years), a home that is worth less than is owed on it. This scenario can be devastating, especially if the couple needs to sell the home quickly or unexpectedly.

Although financial responsibility may sound relatively easy, it isn't. That doesn't mean it is excessively difficult or that you can't do it because you certainly can – no matter how bad your finances are or how much debt you have. Let me say that again. It doesn't matter who you are or how bad your finances appear to be, they can be fixed and there is always hope. The only requirement is that you have to spend less than you make and use the excess to pay off debt. The difficult part of this process is to be conservative with your spending and the way to accomplish this is to clearly identify what is needed and separate those things from the things you want or would like to have. This is the purpose of the spending plan. You may be asking, "What do I do in the case of an emergency?" Most financial advisors and educators state that the first step to financial freedom (even before paying off the debt) is to create an emergency savings of approximately $1,000. This account is then used (instead of credit cards) when the refrigerator breaks, the washing machine starts leaking, the car needs a new transmission, or some other emergency arises. Keep in mind however, that this account is for unexpected emergencies. Normal wear and tear, maintenance, and replacement costs should be accounted for over time in the spending plan.

Another secret to achieving financial freedom is to pay yourself first. This means that you must put some money into savings or investments each month and that you should do this first, in accordance with your spending plan. Even if you have to start with only $20 or $25 a month, you must begin now. You will be surprised how fast this money grows, as long as you don't touch it. Once you get your financial situation stabilized, I recommend that you establish medium and long term savings (in addition to the emergency fund already discussed). The medium savings is used for things like family trips, making home improvements, or purchasing special gifts. Long term savings is used typically for large expenditures such as making a down payment on a new car, house, vacation property etc. Couples should seek to establish a long-term savings of 3-6 months expenses for a rainy day. This can include a period of unemployment, a natural disaster, or a hospitalization. In addition to the savings described above, it is also beneficial for the couple to establish a long-term investment strategy. This can include such things as a 401K, ROTH IRA for retirement, and 529 education funds, as well as other mutual funds, stocks, and/or CDs to be used for education, retirement, or other major expenditures. Again, the key is not the amount, but rather, to simply get started and maintain consistency in the process.

Many couples feel that they must be debt-free prior to investing; if they do this, there is a good chance that they will never actually invest a single penny. It is also important however, that you don't invest more than you can reasonably afford. Investing can be similar to gambling psychologically and it is extremely easy to get carried away. In addition to the things already discussed, it is important for couples to communicate regularly regarding their finances and the progress that is being made. They should establish financial goals and meet together every 3-4 months to see how they are progressing. The couple should critically review each goal in an open and honest way without assigning blame. Additionally, they will need to determine who will be responsible for actually paying the bills and managing the financial records. This is extremely important since a critical part of getting out of debt and obtaining financial freedom is to ensure that all bills are paid on time. This will help to build credit and eliminate late fees.

In addition to the practical aspects of financial planning and management, the couple must work extremely hard to assess, evaluate, and even change their attitudes regarding money, wealth, and finances. Couples spend so much time arguing about finances that the resultant tension, anger, and resentment serve as a wall, barrier, and obstacle to intimacy. Couples must decide for themselves that a marriage is worth more than any amount of money. In other words, when couples come to the realization that if they work together; if they don't obsess over the financial stress they are experiencing; and they sincerely seek to improve their financial situation – then they can and will achieve financial freedom. As couples do this, they have the potential of discovering and establishing real closeness within their relationship – and a true sense of intimacy as a result.

As I stated earlier, my wife and I have fought about finances a lot in the 25+ years that we have been married. That changed recently – not because we became wealthy or that our financial situation suddenly changed, but rather, because we decided that our marriage and each other were more important. What is most amazing to me personally is that once we made that decision, our marriage improved and with time, so have our finances. Marriage is about love and as the saying goes, "happiness can't be bought." Money and the stress that comes with it have the potential to do more harm to a marriage than good. I remember very clearly the early days of my own marriage and the happiness that my wife and I felt as we spent time together getting to know each other and falling deeper in love with one another each and every day. We didn't have much from a material perspective, but we also didn't have an abundance of bills and almost no debt. What we did have was love and happiness. I also remember a couple of years later when we received our first credit card. How I wish we had been better prepared for that responsibility. We were immature and we spent foolishly based on emotion and want as opposed to rational thinking and need. That behavior had a negative impact on our marital relationship. Fortunately, with a lot of hard work and divine intervention, things are going very well. I sometimes wonder though - how much better our marriage and our finances would be had we not been financially irresponsible in the first place.

Figure 1 – Monthly Spending Plan

Area	January	February	March	April	May	June
Rent / mortgage						
Car Payment						
Gasoline						
Car care / maintenance						
Groceries						
Car insurance						
Electricity						
Water						
Trash						
Entertainment						
School						
Clothes						
Home improvement						
Gifts						
Credit Card						
Credit card						
Store Credit						
Life insurance						
Pet expenses						

Figure 2 – Debt Power Pay Example

Month	Car $400	Credit Card #1 $100	Credit Card #2 ($100)	Store #1 ($50)	Store #2 ($50)
January	$400	$100	$100	$50	$50 + 200 = $250
February	$400	$100	$100	$50	$250
March	$400	$100	$100	$50	$250
April	$400	$100	$100	$50	$250
May	$400	$100	$100	$50 + $250 = $300	
June	$400	$100	$100	$300	
July	$400	$100	$100	$300	
August	$400	$100	$300 + $100 = $400		
September	$400	$100	$400		
October	$400	$400 + $100 = $500			
November	$400 + 500 = $900				
December	$900				

FINANCES

Couple Exercise

Instructions: Answer the following questions as completely and honestly as possible. Do not share your answers with your spouse until both of you have finished answering these questions.

1. Describe your family of origin with regards to finances and money. What were your parent's attitudes about money, spending, and debt? Who made the financial or spending decisions? Who paid the bills and managed the finances?

_____

_____

_____

_____

_____

_____

_____

_____

_____

_____

_____

_____

_____

_____

_____

_____

_____

_____

_____

_____

_____

_____

_____

_____

2. Would you describe yourself as financially responsible? Y // N Why or why not?

_____

_____

_____

_____

_____

_____

_____

_____

_____

_____

_____

_____

_____

_____

_____

_____

_____

_____

_____

_____

_____

_____

_____

_____

_____

_____

_____

_____

_____

3. Would you describe your spouse as financially responsible? Y // N Why or why not?

_____

_____

_____

_____

_____

_____

_____

_____

_____

_____

_____

_____

_____

_____

_____

_____

_____

_____

_____

_____

_____

_____

_____

_____

_____

_____

_____

_____

_____

_____

_____

_____

_____

_____

4. Describe your personal financial goals.

_____

_____

_____

_____

_____

_____

_____

_____

_____

_____

_____

_____

_____

_____

_____

_____

_____

_____

_____

_____

_____

_____

_____

_____

_____

_____

_____

_____

_____

_____

_____

_____

_____

5. Have you and your spouse sat down and discussed your specific financial goals? Y // N If so, do you regularly assess your progress in reaching these goals? Y // N Describe how discussing finances with your spouse makes you feel. What is it about this process that makes you feel this way?

_____

_____

_____

_____

_____

_____

_____

_____

_____

_____

_____

_____

_____

_____

_____

_____

_____

_____

_____

_____

_____

_____

_____

_____

_____

_____

_____

_____

_____

_____

_____

_____

_____

_____

6. What would you like to see done differently in your home with regards to money, finances, spending, and debt? What would it take for this to actually happen?

_____

_____

_____

_____

_____

_____

_____

_____

_____

_____

_____

_____

_____

_____

_____

_____

_____

_____

_____

_____

_____

_____

_____

_____

_____

_____

_____

_____

_____

_____

_____

_____

_____

7. Describe the impact money has had on your marriage?

_____

_____

_____

_____

_____

_____

_____

_____

_____

_____

_____

_____

_____

_____

_____

_____

_____

_____

_____

_____

_____

_____

_____

_____

_____

_____

_____

_____

_____

_____

_____

_____

_____

8. (If applicable) What have you taught your children about money and financial responsibility? What changes do you intend to make in this area?

_____

_____

_____

_____

_____

_____

_____

_____

_____

_____

_____

_____

_____

_____

_____

_____

_____

_____

_____

_____

_____

_____

_____

_____

_____

_____

_____

_____

_____

_____

_____

_____

_____

_____

_____

Now that you have answered these questions, sit down with your spouse and discuss each of these questions and how you answered them. Pay particular attention to needs, feelings, and messages that are developed through the discussion.

<u>Action Plan</u>: As a couple, we have decided to make the following changes or to start doing the following things with regards to finances: We will sit down and discuss our progress on this plan in 4 weeks.

(Date and time of next meeting) _____

_____

_____

_____

_____

_____

_____

_____

_____

_____

_____

_____

_____

_____

_____

_____

_____

_____

_____

_____

_____

_____

_____

_____

_____

_____

_____

_____

_____

CHAPTER THREE

Extended Family Relationships

Some of you reading this book may be surprised to learn that relationships with extended family, particularly parents and in-laws can be a significant source of stress for a young married couple. Others may not be surprised at all. In this chapter, I will discuss the dynamics of family relationships that make the extended family situation so stressful. I will also identify methods and tools that will make it easier for couples to deal with the stress of this situation. Finally, I will discuss the issue of caring for the physical well-being of aging parents and how couples can manage this difficult task while also preserving their own marriage in the process. Let the journey begin...

Take the case of Justin and Kimberly. They have been married for just under a year. They are both from neighboring towns and attended the same high school. Following graduation from college, Justin took a job that required him and Kimberly to relocate to a state more than a thousand miles away from their families. For Justin, this has been an exciting move and he is extremely happy with his professional life at work. He enjoys the company he works for, has made many good friends, and loves the challenging work assignments he has been given thus far. Kimberly, on the other hand, is very lonely and dissatisfied. She misses her family and friends and feels isolated from the world. She thought that she and Justin would be spending a lot of time together after he graduated, but the demands put on him at work have made that almost impossible. She and Justin have been fighting and arguing more frequently and it is clear that neither of them is truly happy in the marriage. Justin gets extremely upset at Kimberly because, as he puts it, "she is just being selfish and immature, always calling her mom each and every time we have a disagreement." He feels that Kimberly is shutting him out and instead of coming to him, runs to her mom for comfort, sympathy, and validation.

The situation that Justin and Kimberly are experiencing is not an uncommon one. Many individuals feel that their spouse includes his or her parents in their issues way too much. They feel as though the parents have, in many ways, become part of the marriage - as if they are right there in the room. The individual is enmeshed with his or her parents and the boundaries within the couple relationship have deteriorated or collapsed. Although it isn't always the wife who involves the parents in the disagreement, this is more often than not the typical pattern. Imagine for a minute, that every time you and your spouse get into an argument or gets upset at you for something you have or haven't done, he or she picks up the phone and calls his or her parents. If you are like most people, this will upset you greatly and with time, will become a major source of frustration and contention within the marital relationship. You will likely find yourself feeling shut out, wondering why your spouse has to go running to his or her parents as opposed to just talking to you. Thoughts such as 'why do I bother?" or "why should I even try?" typically come up.

Intrusion on the part of extended family members is not limited to disagreements; it can be an issue in a variety of situations. Planning a birthday, wedding, or other celebration or family event is a common example. I see it in my job as a Chaplain in the military when a young wife is planning an intimate homecoming for her husband following his deployment to Iraq or Afghanistan, only to have his parents demand to be there or perhaps even worse, show up without warning. Either way, it is inappropriate. The couple needs time alone, to bond, and to readjust to life as a married couple.

Why do individuals allow their parents or other extended family members to take such an active role in their marriage, to interfere with the relationship, or to become part of every relational issue within the marriage? The answer to this question is a complex and dynamic one and is not necessarily the same from couple to couple. Many young couples have difficulty communicating, especially regarding issues that are troublesome, emotional, or those that they fear will undoubtedly lead to an argument. They will consciously or even subconsciously do all they can to avoid entering into a conversation with their spouse regarding the parental intrusion. They would simply rather ignore the problem. The spouse however, will likely persist, ultimately to the point that the other person withdraws completely or reacts defensively – at which point the conversation erupts into an argument.

The parents, wanting to protect their child and in an effort to show him or her their love; will listen, validate the emotions that are being shared, and will even go so far as to take sides, pitting their child against his or her spouse. They may take sides, joining against the spouse, even when there has been no wrong-doing. This sends the message to the child that he or she is right and their spouse is wrong. The spouse will likely feel abandoned, alone, criticized, and blamed. He or she is likely to feel that there is no other option but to run, leaving the apartment or home, seeking refuge with a friend or former lover, or even filing for legal separation or divorce. Instead of retreating, he or she may lash out against the other spouse, responding aggressively to these feelings of betrayal and abandonment. This is also the point where thoughts of being single or with someone else begin to surface. Many refer to this as "the grass is greener on the other side of the fence" thinking. It is a dangerous thing and can really become a catalyst for relationship destruction.

The reason the two spouses have failed to interact with one another during this difficult time is because they are afraid to face the tough issues, or have not learned how to communicate, to dialog appropriately, and to solve problems together in a way that allows both partners to feel validated, heard, understood, and satisfied with the outcome. Young couples are sometimes afraid of fighting, of losing an argument, of making their spouse angry. They consciously or subconsciously tell themselves that they will be better off by avoiding the issue, stuffing it inside, or ignoring the problem in hopes that it will simply disappear. Couples operating in this mode are operating under the philosophy "out of sight, out of mind." Unfortunately, most couples find that this strategy does not work and typically actually makes things worse.

It is possible that the individual feels the need for empathy, sympathy, and emotional validation in the course of daily life events, but hasn't learned or is unwilling to turn to their spouse for these things. The person then does what he or she has learned to do over the course of many years – to go to mom and dad for these things. Every time this happens, the relationship between the parents is strengthened or reinforced and the couple relationship is damaged in the process. The couple needs to develop an attachment bond between themselves where they can trust that the other will be there for them and where they can turn to each other and ask for their emotional needs to be met.

It is also possible that the individual, in an attempt to not rock the boat or go against his or her parents, will ignore the issue completely and act as if nothing has happened (similar to what he or she did with the spouse). This time however, the person is afraid to confront the parents, simply hoping that they will stop intruding on their own or that the issue will somehow magically disappear. Unfortunately, this typically does not happen. The person, afraid to confront the parents, comes across to the spouse as unsupportive, weak, lacking courage or confidence, and unreliable. It can cause the spouse to question who is more important – the parents or the spouse, and it can make it difficult to trust him or her in the future. Some clinicians and researchers refer to this as an attachment injury. Couples want to feel loved and supported and they need to know that they are the most important person in each other's lives and that they can rely upon and completely trust each other no matter what.

Given the fact that this way of interacting is typical or commonplace for many couples, the obvious question becomes, "what do we do about it?" I believe that couples must begin by pointing out the tendency to do this to themselves and to each other. If the wife finds herself turning to her parents every time she and her husband have an argument, a big fight, or are experiencing difficulty in their marital relationship, she should begin by telling herself what she has noticed. She should then turn to her husband, telling him what she has discovered. If she fails to notice the behavior, but the husband does, he should gently point out the observed behavior to his wife. The couple can now dialog and discuss this issue and how it is impacting their marriage. It is at this point that they are positioned to make a change and start doing things differently. It is important for couples to recognize that neither spouse wants to hurt the other, but they are likely in survival mode, operating from a defensive posture. They are simply doing what they have learned to do. Deep down they want to experience joy, happiness, and love; but they are stuck, unsure of what to do next – so they simply react. They have to literally learn new ways of interacting with those they love the most.

The couple must begin by realizing that they are now a couple; that they have come together as one and subsequently, no longer exist simply as individuals. They are united in love and in purpose. They are stronger because they have each other. Together they can succeed, prevail, and endure; divided or alone they will likely fall. Although they still have individual likes, dislikes, interests, and goals, they recognize the need for unity – the concept of we or us as opposed to I or me. Some refer to it as synergy, or the idea that "two heads are better than one." In a strong marriage, the husband and wife make each other stronger than they could ever be alone.

This concept of couple then transfers over to the problems and issues that the couple experience in their daily lives together. They need to develop the mindset that "we are now a couple" and that "together we must solve our own problems and differences." This does not mean that they can't solicit advice, guidance, or seek out suggestions, but rather, they recognize that in the end, it is up to them as a couple to work through whatever issues have surfaced within the relationship. The parents, siblings, and close friends are not part of the family system and therefore, do not have a place at the table. It is the couple, and the couple alone that must come together and begin working through the issues at hand.

Once the couple recognizes the fact that they must work together to solve their problems, they will find themselves in a position to do exactly that. They must however, also deal with the fears they have of actually confronting the problems and issues at hand. They need to voice these fears to each other, gain reassurance that they are in a safe place and then when it is all over, they will be in a much better place - as individuals, and as a couple. People are hesitant to enter into discussions about sensitive or problematic areas of the relationship because it makes them feel vulnerable. They must be made to feel safe. This implies that if they feel safe, they will then take the risk of being vulnerable without the fear that their vulnerability will be exposed. They must also experience confidence that regardless of the issue, how invested they or their spouse might be, or how passionate each of them feels about the issue, in the end they will be able to find common ground. This common ground will enable them to reach a compromise, while respecting the outcome as well as the position of their spouse. They must be mature enough to recognize that they can agree to disagree. Resolution does not always mean that the two agree on the issue. They agree on the solution and they agree that their relationship, their love, and their marriage are more important than simply winning an argument.

When dealing with parents, siblings, other family members, and close friends, it is important to recognize that they probably have the best of intentions. They want for you to be happy. They simply do not understand the issue and are far too close to be objective. That being said however, it is critical that you, as a couple, sit down with all applicable parties in an expression of love, telling them how much they are appreciated, how grateful you are for their concern and support; but in no uncertain terms, you must also let them know that it is you who must deal with the issues. It is your marriage and you need to be allowed the space to do what you must do as a couple to work through whatever issues and problems arise. This will be difficult to do and will require considerable courage. In the end however, it will pave the road for success in the marriage.

Caring For Aging Parents

People are living longer than ever before. While modern medicine, increased health awareness, and perhaps better lifestyle choices have extended the life expectation of both men and women in the United States, it has also increased the likelihood that we will possibly have to support and care for our parents and/or our spouse's parents. This is a difficult situation for couples and families to be in since it places enormous stress on the family system while also producing significant personal or individual stress. It is not uncommon for couples to have their own parents living with them while their own children are still living at home. This is sometimes referred to as the "sandwich generation." Increasing numbers of adult children are also moving back home due to financial difficulties and hardships. Many of these adult children are in their 30s and 40s. Related to the previous chapter on finances, couples typically do not develop financial plans that include caring for their parents or adult children. The emotional and even spiritual impact of the situation is also oftentimes grossly underestimated.

One of the more common interpersonal situations taking place when a couple finds themselves needing to take care of aging parents is reluctance or resistance on the part of the other spouse. This resistance can be expressed in many different ways ranging from a verbalized "absolutely not!" to more passive-aggressive comments and behaviors. This resistance can be either conscious and deliberate or even subconscious. The spouse wanting to care for the parents is left feeling alone, unsupported, and maybe even unloved. They will then have difficulty trusting their spouse, feeling that he or she won't be there for them in the future. The other spouse will feel that their husband or wife is choosing the parent(s) over him or her. This makes them question the relationship, the marriage, and whether the spouse actually loves him or her. The spouse will feel that they are secondary to the parent(s) and will usually feel neglected as well. This will then result in lowered feelings of self-worth and could ultimately lead to problems with depression. The cognitive belief here is "I don't matter," "I am worthless," or "I am not important to him (her)." It also makes it extremely difficult for the couple to enjoy time with each other and may preclude them from going out or taking vacations together. The intimacy within the relationship is likely to be severely impacted over time. This, in turn, may lead one of the two partners to seek escape or relief elsewhere. Common outlets become work, hobbies, alcohol, the children, or even an affair. The dynamic is such that the spouse responds to the situation at home by withdrawing towards something or someone else.

Knowing that this situation is not uncommon and could happen to any of us, it is important for couples to adequately prepare and to give thought to how they might handle it. The couple must get on the same page regarding their willingness or lack thereof to actually care for their aging parents. Some people think that if there are multiple siblings, each will contribute or take a turn in helping. This simply is not the case. Responsibility will oftentimes fall upon the oldest child; the male child; the closest; the wealthiest; or even the one with the most experience in the area of nursing, health care, or human services. They might say something such as "you are a nurse; it only makes sense that you take care of mom. You know what to do way more than me." Responsibility can also fall upon the stay-at-home mom. The implication being that she is at home anyways and has nothing but time. Some may even justify it by adding, "You will both enjoy the company." This puts great pressure on the individual and the couple and makes them feel that they are alone and have been abandoned in the care-taking role. It is therefore important for siblings to discuss this before the parents actually need the care. Considerations include finances, time, logistics, level of required care, and other pertinent concerns. The siblings also need to include their spouses in the discussion as the ultimate decision will have significant impact on them as well. The parents should be consulted as to their wishes and they should make it clear as to what they desire and what resources they might have to alleviate the financial burden on the children.

For the couple taking on this important and sacred care-taking role, it is important that they fully discuss the implications. They need to realize that there may or may not be a financial cost depending on contributions from other family members and how well prepared the parents were in planning their state for retirement. The couple must discuss changes that will need to be made to accommodate the potential financial aspects of the arrangement. This is especially important if they have children preparing for college or if other costly transitions are on the horizon. If the parents aren't careful, the children could feel that they are being deprived of things that they feel they are entitled to. This may subsequently cause them to feel a sense of resentment towards their grandparents. Couples must therefore incorporate the financial aspects of caring for parents into their retirement plans and must be prepared in case the need arises before they are ready. These needs can happen with or without warning. An example of this might be the need for additional care following a stroke, heart attack, or confirmation of a chronic illness. In other words, there may not be any preliminary indications of an impending need and there subsequently may not be time later to plan.

In addition to the financial aspects of the decision, it is important for couples to discuss the psychological and emotional aspects of the decision. Both spouses need to support each other in the decision and be made to feel that this is in fact, a joint decision. Not doing so will result in feelings of betrayal, abandonment, isolation, resentment, and exclusion on the part of both spouses. Once the decision is made and agreed upon, it is vital that the couple realize that they are a couple and that just as when they had young children in the home, they are the most important relationship in the home. They must preserve their marriage and their identity as a couple. They must spend time together – alone. This may involve having to hire someone to care for the elderly parent(s). If there are older children at home, it is possible that they could take on some of this responsibility. The couple must go out together, have fun together, and even travel places together for short periods of time. They must take vacations and find hobbies that they can share together. This process of maintaining the couple identity and spending time together will help to preserve the marriage as well as other relationships within the home.

It is also important for the parents to spend time with the children when possible. The easiest way to accomplish this is by making these things routine and consistently making them a part of one's daily, weekly, and monthly schedule. In a sense, the couple and the family (if there are still children at home) must learn to pay themselves first in terms of spending time together. This won't necessarily be easy however and the couple must be proactive in identifying community and social support. There are agencies that provide respite care and depending on level of need, it is possible that a neighbor, friend, or other family member can fill in from time to time as well.

The important element when dealing with extended family is to remember that you, as a couple, are vitally important and that you must be deliberate in your actions to preserve the couple relationship. Prior planning is a necessity and the more prepared you can be, the better things are likely to turn out. I would recommend adapting the philosophy "plan for the worst and hope for the best."

EXTENDED FAMILY

Couple Exercise

Instructions: Answer the following questions as completely and honestly as possible. Do not share your answers with your spouse until both of you have finished answering these questions.

1. Do you currently feel that family members and/or friends are over-involved in your marital relationship? Y // N If so, describe how this is occurring and how it has made you feel.

_____

_____

_____

_____

_____

_____

_____

_____

_____

_____

_____

_____

_____

_____

_____

_____

_____

_____

_____

_____

_____

2. What changes would you like to see made with regards to the involvement of extended family or others in your marital relationship?

_____

_____

_____

_____

_____

_____

_____

_____

_____

_____

_____

_____

_____

_____

_____

_____

_____

_____

_____

_____

_____

_____

_____

_____

_____

_____

_____

_____

_____

_____

_____

_____

_____

_____

_____

_____

3. What have you done to prepare for the possibility of having to care for aging parents? Address physical, financial, and emotional aspects of this planning as applicable.

_____
_____
_____
_____
_____
_____
_____
_____
_____
_____
_____
_____
_____
_____
_____
_____
_____
_____
_____
_____
_____
_____
_____
_____
_____
_____
_____
_____
_____
_____
_____
_____

4. What are your perceptions regarding your spouse's feelings pertaining to caring for aging parents or other extended family members? What are his or her feelings regarding allowing adult children to live at home? Contrast these perceptions with your own thoughts on these questions.

Now that you have answered these questions, sit down with your spouse and discuss each of these questions and how you answered them. Pay particular attention to needs, feelings, and messages that are developed through the discussion.

<u>Action Plan</u>: As a couple, we have decided to make the following changes or to start doing the following things with regards to extended family issues: We will sit down and discuss our progress on this plan in 4 weeks.

(Date and time of next meeting) _____

_____

_____
_____
_____
_____
_____
_____
_____
_____
_____
_____
_____
_____
_____
_____
_____
_____
_____
_____
_____
_____
_____
_____
_____
_____
_____
_____
_____
_____

CHAPTER FOUR

Healthy Sexuality & Intimacy

Sex is one of those things that couples often argue about, or worse yet, avoid discussing at all. I would like to begin this chapter by saying that I firmly believe that sex is part of a healthy relationship and that a sexual relationship develops and changes over time based on many different physical and emotional factors. I will add to this that great sex, perhaps even good sex, requires some level of intimacy. That does not mean that couples always have sex for emotional reasons or that they don't sometimes have sex just for the physical satisfaction of the experience. What I am saying is that purely physical sex should not be the norm and that sex that includes intimacy will almost always be more satisfying to both partners. So when it comes to sex, what do couples typically argue about and what kinds of things should they be discussing?

One of the common dynamics I see with the couples I have worked with is disagreement over the frequency of sex. We typically think that this involves a couple where the man constantly wants to have sex and the wife doesn't. Interestingly enough, in my experience, these roles are often reversed. Regardless of who wants it more, the real problem is that there is a difference in need or desire. There is no right answer to the question of "how often should a couple be having sex?" It is not uncommon for couples to disagree about how often they should have sex, but they need to come together and discuss this issue as opposed to ignoring it or blaming each other. The wife will sometimes say "he is a sex maniac…he wants nothing but sex, all the time." He will then reply "at least I want sex… you never do." This short interchange is about two people who are feeling hurt, rejected, unloved, unappreciated, and disrespected. Instead of discussing these feelings however, they quickly turn it into blame, criticism, resentment, and defensiveness.

A typical message delivered by a couple as they interact goes something like this: The husband will begin to communicate to his wife that he wants sex – oftentimes this is accomplished by touching or fondling her, kissing her, or teasing her by playing with her breasts or butt. As he persists however, she starts to feel that she is nothing more than a sexual object to him. She may begin to wonder if he even sees her as a real person – someone or something beyond the sexual parts. In the most extreme cases, she may feel like a prostitute or human sex doll. She subsequently starts to feel less important, worthwhile or valued. She then tells him no. She tells him that she does not want to have sex. He hears "I am rejecting you." He perceives the situation to be about him. He may think "there is something wrong with me." He may even hear her saying "you are not desirable, attractive, or appealing to me." He begins to feel rejected and unloved. He may even wonder if she is having an affair, possibly accusing

45

her of such actions; subsequently causing the conversation to escalate out of control. All of these things bring up additional insecurities, as well as feelings of hopelessness and worthlessness.

What is interesting – and sad is the fact that these perceived messages are a far cry from the intended message which could be "honey, I find you extremely wonderful and desirable. You are my partner in life and I would like nothing better than to make love to you." The intended message may have been "it has been a really hard day and although I love you with all my heart, I really don't feel excited about making love right now. I am sure I will later though." One scenario is filled with blame, rejection, hopelessness, and bitterness; while the other contains feelings of love, understanding, and acceptance. Which would you rather have?

When couples complain about a difference in sex drive or differences in desired frequency, I ask them if that has always been the case or if there has ever been a time when things were better. If the difference in desired frequency is something new, I focus on things that may have changed. It is important to note that changes in desire oftentimes occur with age, following the birth of children, while pregnant, and when one is extremely tired or experiencing significant stress. There may also be a medical reason and therefore, it is always a good idea to consult your doctor or get a physical just to rule out organic causes. The next step is to look at stress. What is going on in your life individually and as a couple that might be causing distress? Maybe the wife is home taking care of the children all day and by the time she and her husband are ready for bed, she is simply exhausted. It is difficult for anyone to be interested in sex or making love when they are exhausted. Husbands can assist with this situation by coming home and making a conscientious effort to help his wife so that they can go to bed together and so she will be less tired. The wife is also going to feel very appreciative of the husband's efforts and want to connect with him. Guys, get the hint here…this means that she may be more interested in having sex with you if you are more helpful around the house and with the children. Take care of the dishes or the children yourself and let her go take a warm bath. Better yet, prepare the bath for her. It might be helpful to the relationship to plan other times besides evenings and nights to make love. Many couples have commented that they enjoy sex in the mornings (perhaps after getting the kids off to school). If one of the parents stays home, maybe the other can come home for an extended lunch break or take the afternoon off all together.

Other stressors such as financial problems, troubled work relationships, and other marital problems can also cause stress that could likely result in diminished sexual desire. These specific things must then be identified and dealt with separately as appropriate. In situations such as these, the sexual relationship incorrectly becomes the focus or the main issue when in reality, it is these other stressors. In other words, if money issues are causing a problem sexually for the couple, sex is not the problem – money is. Sex is the symptom of a bigger problem – one that must be dealt with quickly and thoroughly.

Another thing couples argue or fight about related to sex is when to have children and how many to have. This is a critical question and is one that is best discussed prior to actually getting married. I am amazed at the large number of couples who have been married a year or two only to discover that there are considerable differences in this area. The husband may say that he wants a large family, possibly as many as five or six children. To which she replies, "We never discussed children. I want a career.

I may never want to have children. I definitely don't want five or six." This creates a real problem as it shatters the couple's expectations or view of what they thought marred life would look like. They may feel that this isn't the person that they married and may even feel lied to and betrayed. If something happens and the wife becomes pregnant there may also be suspicions that she got pregnant on purpose and "sabotaged the birth control process." The bottom line is that if a couple finds themselves in this situation, they should seek professional counseling. They will need assistance in discussing and resolving this dilemma. It can be done, but it will be a difficult and challenging process.

In addition to the very important issues discussed so far, couples also argue and fight about what is or is not acceptable in the bedroom. As technology develops, society becomes more encouraging of (or at least less resistant to) sexual curiosity and trying new things. Couples may find themselves in a situation where they disagree about something they are considering doing or trying. For example, the husband may want them to watch porn together. One or the other may want to perform or receive oral sex or to try anal sex. They may want to incorporate toys such as dildos or vibrators, or they may even suggest including a third person or even swapping with another couple. This discussion is not meant to be a moral debate as much as it is an issue of communication and respect. All individuals have sexual fantasies and are curious about trying something new or different. That being said however, I believe that the decision must be mutual. Couples should discuss their fantasies and desires with one another, but in a way that is not offensive, or demeaning. They must agree on the things they are going to do. If one partner says no then it simply doesn't happen. It should also not be something that humiliates the other person, hurts them, or causes them any unnecessary or unwanted pain.

It is also important however, for spouses to listen to each other and make reasonable attempts to please and satisfy each other. I often ask people "Who should make the decision as to what happens in the bedroom?" Many men will indicate that they should. Many men falsely believe that they are in control and therefore should make all decisions. The desired goal, as stated earlier however, is that couples should make that decision together. To accomplish this task and have a wonderful and satisfying sex life, couples must talk to each other about sex. I know this may sound a little strange, but couples, for many different reasons, are reluctant to talk to each other about sex. I ask couples why they are willing to have conversations about hundreds of topics in just about every room of the house, but are unwilling to have a discussion in the bedroom (or anywhere else for that matter) about sex.

Intimacy is enhanced when couples discuss and talk about sex, especially with reference to their fantasies and desires. Couples sometimes mistakenly believe that sex is a dirty or taboo topic. In reality however, it is just the opposite. It is a beautiful and important part of the relationship. Couples need to realize this and not be afraid to discuss their sexuality. They also need to affirm each other's worthiness or desirability as a man, woman, and lover. Couples should strive to complement each other and to get excited when they see each other. I often hear women say "he doesn't look at me the way he used to." Men and women should also recognize that looking at other men and women is demeaning to their partner. Don't pretend - you know what I am talking about. Most of us are guilty of this...once in a while at least. I want you to notice the pain in your partner's eyes the next time you "check out" another person in front of them. Looking at someone else in a lustful way makes the other feel inferior, not as pretty or sexy, and destroys their self-esteem. It also makes them question whether or not you might actually cheat and if you would rather be with someone else. These actions and subsequent feelings will result in a loss of intimacy and a distancing within the relationship.

A topic related to sex that is extremely important for us to discuss and one that many people oftentimes actually mistakenly take to mean the same thing as sex is that of intimacy. When someone says that they are intimate with another person, we assume they are saying that they are in a sexual relationship with that individual. In actuality however, we are in intimate relationships with a lot of different people and most of those are not sexual. Intimacy is about closeness or the establishment of an emotional relationship or bond. We can be intimate with a good friend because we share various parts of our lives together and we share with each other many of our most personal thoughts and feelings.

Military service members that serve together, particularly in combat where they are relying on one another for survival, are usually quite intimate with one another. Sibling relationships and parent-child relationships are another example of intimate relationships. Even co-workers can form intimate relationships as they share time together working on projects, oftentimes discussing personal goals, dreams, and aspirations. In other words, intimacy involves emotional connectedness or closeness, as well as trust and respect. We should seek to establish these things most in our marriages. The problem is that many of us don't truly know what intimacy looks like and did not have it modeled for us as children or adolescents growing up. Therefore, we "wing it", trying to do the best we can without a roadmap or set of instructions.

So what does this discussion of intimacy have to do with you and your spouse and your sexual relationship? Husbands and wives should be best friends and by virtue of that relationship, should have a level of intimacy and closeness unlike any other. They should be able to be completely honest, transparent, and comfortable with one another. An individual should be able to stand naked (literally and metaphorically) in front of their spouse with no worries of embarrassment, shame, or humiliation. In fact they should do so with the belief that their spouse appreciates them as a person which includes their physical body. They should also feel comfortable sharing feelings, thoughts, opinions, and beliefs with each other. This is difficult for many men to do, yet it is what most women so desperately want and feel they need from their husband. Most women (more so than men) also feel that they need to be emotionally connected to a man or have an intimate relationship with him prior to having sex or making love. Therefore, intimacy is vitally important for her and if a man wants to be able to make love to his wife, he needs to help establish intimacy in that relationship.

The obvious next question for the couple then becomes, "how do we establish this intimate relationship?" It begins with simply spending time together - doing things together and sharing life experiences. Couples should spend time (not necessarily all their time however) doing things that they both enjoy and enjoy doing together. Not all couples are going to agree on every activity so it is important to compromise and sometimes do something for the other person simply because you love them and want to spend time with them. This is why women will sometimes sit and watch a football game or a NASCAR race with their husband. My wife does this for me and I truly appreciate it...even if she doesn't really understand what is happening. Similarly, many husbands will agree to attend a class with their wife, going for walks with their wife, attending a musical, or taking their wife to the gym even though doing so may lower the overall intensity of the workout. This communicates to the other person that they are important and perhaps just as importantly, that the relationship is important. It is about spending time together, sharing experiences, and building memories.

On a similar note, couples need to have a date-night every week. This means going out, just the two of them – without the children. I realize this may be difficult for many reasons, but you, your spouse, and your marriage deserve it. You also need to get away overnight together. This may be more difficult, but incorporate it into your budget, save for it, find a good babysitter (if applicable), and make it happen at least once a quarter. If babysitting is a problem, meet other couples and once you feel comfortable with them, talk to them about trading baby-sitting responsibilities. This avoids the financial burden of baby-sitting all together. Dates don't have to be expensive and don't have to involve going out to a fancy restaurant or seeing a movie. In fact, the best dates are those that involve more interaction and opportunities to talk and connect. A fun way to make the date-night even more romantic is to take turns planning the activity, only sharing enough information with your spouse that he or she knows when to be ready and what to wear. The key is to have fun and put your spouse first. Make him or her feel that they are the most important person in your life. I have had so many women tell me that they only wish that their husbands would treat them as though they truly mattered - that nothing was more important.

Another way that couples can increase their level of intimacy is to take time out of their day on a consistent basis to sit and actually talk to each other. This doesn't have to take a lot of time. Taking 20-60 minutes a day just to talk to each other will do wonders for the quality of the marriage. You may be thinking we talk at dinner or while watching television. Those conversations may feel sufficient, but they involve distractions. They may seem like enough to you, but are they to your spouse? The kids are oftentimes there at the dinner table and be honest…isn't your mind somewhat distracted by the process of eating? Television is a major distraction as conversations that are held while watching television are rushed and contain an enormous amount of interruptions. You may be surprised how little you actually retain or hear from these conversations. Conversations should be held in a way that couples can actually sit down together, look at one another, and reach out and touch one another. They should also take place in a location void of any distractions. This may be awkward at first, but once couples learn to really talk to each other, the intimacy increases and the couple ends up wanting to talk even more. It feels good because loving someone and being loved by that person feels good. There is nothing better than true intimacy.

Couples sometimes find themselves asking "what are we possibly going to talk about?" If you find yourself in this situation, then there definitely are intimacy issues. Topics to discuss should not be difficult to find and don't have to be about the relationship or something that you are struggling with. Look in the newspaper or on the nightly news for topics. Check internet news sites for stories worthy of discussion. You can also talk about a movie you both saw or a book you recently read. You may also choose to just discuss a question such as the following:

- What would you do with a million dollars?
- What would you do if you discovered you only had a year to live?
- If you could have one wish what would it be?

- If you could change one thing about yourself what would it be?
- What is the most important thing you learned as a child?
- What has been your greatest life challenge?
- What would you like to be doing in 10 or 20 years?
- What is your favorite movie and why?
- If you were President of the United States what would be your top priority?
- Where would you go for vacation if you could go anywhere?
- What do you consider your greatest life accomplishment?
- What do you consider your greatest strength?
- What do you consider your greatest weakness?
- How do you view adversity?
- What distinguishes adversity from challenges?
- Do you believe in luck?

The important point to remember is that you are simply trying to get to know your husband or wife the best you possibly can. You want to know what makes them unique, what makes them tick, and what life experiences have contributed to who they are and what makes them the person you fell in love with. As you do so, the intimacy within the relationship will increase dramatically.

HEALTHY SEXUALITY AND INTIMACY

Couple Exercise

Instructions: Answer the following questions as completely and honestly as possible. Do not share your answers with your spouse until both of you have finished answering these questions.

1. What does intimacy mean to you? Describe its' impact on your marriage (be specific as possible). Rate the level of intimacy in your marriage on a scale of 0-10 (10 being highest).

_____
_____
_____
_____
_____
_____
_____
_____
_____
_____
_____
_____
_____
_____
_____
_____
_____
_____
_____
_____
_____
_____
_____

2. Are you satisfied with the level of intimacy in your marriage Y // N? Why or why not? Do you feel that your spouse is satisfied with the level of intimacy in the marriage Y // N? Why or why not? Describe what things you currently do together for fun and the ways that you spend time together currently.

_____
_____
_____
_____
_____
_____
_____
_____
_____
_____
_____
_____
_____
_____
_____
_____
_____
_____
_____
_____
_____
_____
_____
_____
_____
_____
_____
_____
_____
_____
_____
_____
_____
_____
_____

3. What kinds of things would you like to do together that you aren't currently? How might these things increase the intimacy in your relationship?

_____

_____

_____

_____

_____

_____

_____

_____

_____

_____

_____

_____

_____

_____

_____

_____

_____

_____

_____

_____

_____

_____

_____

_____

_____

_____

_____

_____

_____

_____

_____

_____

_____

_____

_____

_____

_____

_____

_____

4. Describe what you learned about with regards to intimacy and sexuality growing up? How have these lessons impacted you in your marriage?

_____
_____
_____
_____
_____
_____
_____
_____
_____
_____
_____
_____
_____
_____
_____
_____
_____
_____
_____
_____
_____
_____
_____
_____
_____
_____
_____
_____
_____
_____
_____
_____
_____
_____
_____
_____
_____
_____

5. Describe your thoughts regarding the relationship between intimacy and sexuality. What do you like best about the sexual part of your marriage? What would you like to change about it?

_____

_____

_____

_____

_____

_____

_____

_____

_____

_____

_____

_____

_____

_____

_____

_____

_____

_____

_____

_____

_____

_____

_____

_____

_____

_____

_____

_____

_____

_____

_____

_____

_____

_____

_____

_____

_____

_____

_____

_____

_____

6. How often do you and your spouse discuss sex and your sexual relationship? What do these conversations feel like for you? What makes these conversations difficult?

_____
_____
_____
_____
_____
_____
_____
_____
_____
_____
_____
_____
_____
_____
_____
_____
_____
_____
_____
_____
_____
_____
_____
_____
_____
_____
_____
_____
_____
_____
_____
_____
_____
_____
_____

7. Describe your sexual fantasy. Does your spouse know about it Y // N? If not, why? In what ways have you tried to fulfill this fantasy? What could you do with your spouse to fulfill this fantasy?

_____

_____

_____

_____

_____

_____

_____

_____

_____

_____

_____

_____

_____

_____

_____

_____

_____

_____

_____

_____

_____

_____

_____

_____

_____

_____

_____

_____

_____

_____

_____

_____

_____

_____

_____

_____

_____

_____

8. How often do you and your spouse go on a date? How are they planned? What kinds of things do you do? What would you like to change about these dates?

_____
_____
_____
_____
_____
_____
_____
_____
_____
_____
_____
_____
_____
_____
_____
_____
_____
_____
_____
_____
_____
_____
_____
_____
_____
_____
_____
_____
_____
_____
_____
_____
_____
_____

Now that you have answered these questions, sit down with your spouse and discuss each of these questions and how you answered them. Pay particular attention to needs, feelings, and messages that are developed through the discussion.

<u>Action Plan</u>: As a couple, we have decided to make the following changes or to start doing the following things with regards to healthy sexuality and intimacy: We will sit down and discuss our progress on this plan in 4 weeks.

(Date and time of next meeting) _____

_____
_____
_____
_____
_____
_____
_____
_____
_____
_____
_____
_____
_____
_____
_____
_____
_____
_____
_____
_____
_____
_____
_____
_____
_____
_____
_____
_____
_____
_____

CHAPTER FIVE

Infidelity

Infidelity - Why Men and Women Cheat

Since the dawn of time, people have been asking why men and women cheat on each other – on the person they supposedly love and committed to spend the rest of their live with. Every betrayed spouse that I have counseled wants to know and understand why it happened. They ask questions such as "Am I not pretty enough?" "Am I not sexy enough?" "Am I not good enough in bed?" Infidelity, on or offline, is not about physical appearance or strangely enough, even about sex. The focus becomes the sex because that is the observable behavior involved, but the reasons underlying the behavior and the betrayal go much deeper.

Infidelity or cheating can take many different forms and can include a wide range of behaviors such as: pornography (with or without masturbation), chatting online, cybersex, texting, talking with others of the opposite sex on the phone, off-line dates or meetings, off-line (real time) sex, looking at or using online dating sites, having sex with escorts or prostitutes, and going to strip clubs or adult book stores. The most important thing to recognize is that cheating or infidelity is defined by the individual and hopefully the couple as well. That definition varies from individual to individual and couple to couple. It is also important to note that emotional infidelity can be just as devastating as physical infidelity. I had a wife once tell me that her husband had been cheating on her. When I inquired about the behaviors involved, she said that he was chatting online with a woman in another country (a woman he had not met and probably never would meet) and was telling her about his job and what it was like being in the military. The wife had walked into the room, observed the online conversation and told him that he was cheating. He asked how he could be cheating when there was nothing sexual about the conversation. She then told him it was cheating because he was sharing things with another woman that he had never (for whatever reason) shared with her. This is an example of emotional infidelity (as defined by the wife in this case) and for many it is more hurtful than a physical relationship because it involves connectedness that is longed for.

Affairs and other forms of infidelity or cheating can be the result of stress. I have seen many people use sex as a way of self-medicating. A person can use sex to escape life's problems in the same manner they would with alcohol or drugs. Once this happens, a cycle of compulsive behavior or addiction can begin in which the brain starts to use sex as a way to feel good or even normal. I have witnessed couples use sex to escape stress in the marriage – using it as a way to avoid issues and confrontation, and

I have seen individuals use sex to escape various life stressors including legal, financial, job, relationship, family, medical, and even combat.

In addition to trying to escape stressful situations, people also act out sexually or engage in affairs in an attempt to feel close to someone emotionally. This happens more frequently in relationships where the couple spends little time together, have difficulty communicating, or for whatever reason, have failed to connect emotionally on an intimate level. This can be during times of physical separation or it can also be caused by periods of emotional or physical unavailability during such times as the birth of a child, one or both spouses going to school, when both spouses are actively working outside the home, when one of the spouses starts a second job, or when one or both spouses experience an increase in responsibility at work. Community, church, and child activities can also cause a distancing effect on the marriage and subsequently contribute to problems such as infidelity. It is for this reason that couples need to assess their availability to each other and take action to fix the problem if deficiencies are noted. Couples need to discuss these things and be willing to open up to one another regarding their need for the other to be more attentive or accessible.

Another reason that individuals cheat or act out sexually has to do with what is referred to in the counseling or psychology literature as attachment injuries. These injuries are relational in nature and can occur in childhood, adolescence or even adulthood. They have to do with diminished feelings of self-worth and lack of validation by those the person cares most about, relies on, and trusts. Parents, siblings, and romantic partners are the best examples of trusted relationships where attachment injuries most often occur. They subsequently internalize feelings of low self-esteem or worthlessness and learn to not trust others, preventing themselves from getting too close to others as a result - in anticipation of being hurt.

Another cause of infidelity has to do with how they perceive themselves physically and the extent to which they are viewed as desirable by those they associate with. Acting out sexually later in life can be a way of compensating; an attempt to feel good about oneself. Feelings of rejection are minimized and self-esteem enhanced because they are not likely to feel rejected by the woman on the computer screen, the dancer at the local strip club, or even the beautiful escort that is willing to have sex with them (even though it is for money). I have become aware of several married women who have had affairs after undergoing weight-loss surgery. They like the way they look and feel and enjoy the extra attention they are getting from various men. They feel beautiful, sexy, and desirable. In some ways, they feel like a new person and want to experience things that they have possibly never had the opportunity to do as a result of being overweight and self-conscious.

Infidelity can take many different forms and with recent statistics showing that 60% of married men and 40% of married women have had an extramarital sexual relationship, many couples will have to deal with infidelity and its' impact upon their marriage. Infidelity is treatable. Healing may take a lot of work and time, but recovery is possible. Infidelity is a symptom of other significant relationship issues. It forces the couple to look at and deal with problems that have probably been building for quite some time. Once therapy and recovery from the affair is complete the relationship is typically in a very good place - one that many would have never thought possible. I have had couples tell me that in retrospect, the affair was the best thing that happened to their marriage because it forced them to confront the problems, to change the way they interacted with each other, and to learn to love each other and to fall in love with each other all over again. Many couples get married young and don't really understand the commitment and work that is involved in building a strong marriage. They think marriage is just like dating and that it is always joyful and fun. Relationships are difficult and it is hard to live with another person at times. When the going gets tough, many young couples feel that the relationship is just too hard, that they made a mistake, and that there must be something or someone better out there. They will articulate the belief that they deserve to be happy and when an appealing alternative comes along, they quickly abandon ship to pursue newfound opportunities.

Healing from Infidelity

Having presented an overview of some of the common reasons men and women cheat, the next place we need to spend some time is discussing how to deal with infidelity once it has occurred and what couples can do to keep it from happening in the first place. As stated earlier, infidelity is typically the result of many factors building up over the course of time within the relationship. These problems can stem from many different sources, but in all cases, the couple has found themselves unable to effectively deal with these problems. It is not unusual for couples to even fail to recognize the significance of the problems in the first place. In other words, they have adjusted to the situation and have accepted the situation and the problem as the norm. It may be all they know or they may be "living with the situation" out of fear of making things worse.

Infidelity, as stated earlier is about much more than sex. The couple should begin by recognizing this fact and accepting the idea that recovery from infidelity is a difficult, painful, and time consuming process. Depending on the specifics of the particular couple, it is likely to take a year or more for things to be good again in the relationship. It is also possible that things will never be good again. Both spouses need to be honest with themselves and each other and commit to the process only if they are willing to invest themselves in it. What I am saying is that it will be a difficult journey and there are no guarantees. They also need to realize that they got married for a reason, and that they must work hard to rediscover that reason and the feelings that go along with it. One of the goals along the journey of recovery from infidelity may be to fall back in love again. I have seen it happen and it is a beautiful sight. In fact, some relationship experts say that couples should find ways to fall deeper in love each and every day.

The couple should start by realizing that the injured partner (the one who did not have the affair) is extremely hurt. For ease of discussion, we will assume that to be the wife. She will experience significant emotional pain and will feel extremely betrayed. She will question the marriage, the vows that were taken and how those things now fit into her view of the world, relationships and people in general, and her husband and the marriage in particular. She will also question her own self-worth. She will wonder if she has been a good wife, a good lover, and will even ask why she was not good enough or pretty enough to satisfy him. It is important that she seek out individual counseling with a supportive therapist who can empathize and relate to what she is going through without beating up the husband and attacking him in the process. She will have zero trust at this point. This is important so I will say it again. She will not trust him or anything he says or does. This lack of trust is expected and it is normal.

Trust can be rebuilt, but it takes considerable effort and time on the part of both individuals. They both need to be extremely patient with themselves and with one another. The person that had the affair must be an open book, completely transparent with everything he says and does above board and out in the open. He may feel controlled by this but to be perfectly blunt, too bad…get over it. As the husband does this however, trust will begin to be restored and in time, can be back to normal.

The betraying spouse (the one who had the affair) is also hurting. He is likely to feel extremely guilty, ashamed, and scared. You may be thinking that he deserves to be feeling this way, but try to recognize that his behavior is not the only problem that needs to be addressed. There is a reason he cheated. Things were happening with him personally and within the relationship that allowed him to cheat. It was wrong; there is no denying that. If the couple wants to heal, they must work towards understanding these things. There may also be an addiction present. This is especially likely if there have been numerous affairs and/or a progression of sexual behavior to include such things as chatting, compulsive masturbation, patronizing strip clubs, or utilizing the services of prostitutes or escorts. It is important that the betraying spouse seek out a good counselor for individual therapy, particularly one with experience working with infidelity and compulsive sexual behavior. Good resources for finding these therapists include the following: The International Institute for Trauma and Addiction Professionals (www.iitap.com), The Society for the Advancement of Sexual Health (www.sash.net), and The American Association for Marriage and Family Therapy (www.aamft.org).

Once the affair is discovered, the couple is immediately thrown into shock. The wife will likely become very angry, confronting and attacking her husband verbally and possibly even physically. She may leave and go to a friend or family member's house. He will likely deny the affair and either withdraw or assume a defensive position in response to the wife's confrontation. This denial of the affair typically makes things much worse. Usually she already knows and has proof to support the accusations. The denial only makes it harder for the wife to trust her husband again. She may even ask him to leave the house, or he may decide to do that on his own, especially if she has become violent or aggressive. It is important to recognize that violence is never okay and that all possible steps need to be taken to maintain composure and safety in these situations.

Both spouses need a support network that they can engage almost immediately. This is a delicate issue though because the couple must be extremely cautious with regards to whom they allow in. This is an issue that involves great amounts of shame and embarrassment for both spouses. Friends and family members who are likely to tell others without permission should probably not be included as part of the support system or their access to information should be limited. The wife in this case is going to feel like telling her family about the situation and what an evil and horrible thing her husband did and how hurt she is as a result. Avoid doing this. As you begin to work through the infidelity and things get to the point where the relationship is good again, he needs to feel like the wife's parents are not totally against him, that they are not aware of all the details, and that he is not viewed as a monster in their eyes. The parents (on both sides) can be there for encouragement and advice, but the couple must really be careful about how much information is shared. The damage done by doing so can be non-repairable.

Many couples ask if separation is a good idea or not. This is a very personal decision. I can see many advantages and disadvantages to a short separation. Separating for a few days or even a couple of weeks gives both of them an opportunity to deal with the situation and develop a better understanding of their feelings about the infidelity and its impact on their lives. It gives them time to ponder the meaning of the relationship and its future, and to determine what they need from their spouse and the relationship at this point in time. It also establishes a boundary and sends a clear message to the betraying spouse that what he or she did is unacceptable. Regardless of the reason, the affair behavior can't be condoned on any level. The problem is that it is difficult for couples to work on their relationship if they aren't living together. This is why the separation, if there is one, should be short.

Once the separation period is over (assuming there is one), the couple needs to be very clear with their goals for the relationship. They might not be able to say that they want the marriage to work out or that they think it will, but they need to at least say they are willing to try. There is a lot of hurt - on the part of both spouses, and it will take considerable time and effort to heal the pain involved. It is critical that the affair is completely over. The betraying spouse must ensure that all contact with the other person is eliminated. This may be difficult if the other person is a co-worker, family member, or close family friend. Simply put, it doesn't matter. All contact with that person must be ended. This means physical, as well as electronic (e-mail, text messages etc.), phone, and written. The betraying spouse should make sure this is clear to all concerned by putting it in writing and/or making a phone call stating so – with the spouse present if necessary. The important element to this is that the injured partner should be shown the letter / e-mail or be able to listen while the phone call is made. This will give her some small amount of closure and is the first step towards rebuilding trust and finding hope.

The injured partner is likely going to want all the details. This may help some at the beginning, but continuously asking and receiving the specific details of the affair is not going to be therapeutic or helpful. The betraying spouse should be open to giving whatever information is asked for, particularly at the beginning. Keep in mind however, that the injured partner will likely become very upset or agitated upon hearing some of the details. The idea of her husband having sex with another woman is difficult to handle. Couples can easily get to a point where the details of the affair and the affair itself are all that is discussed. If this is happening, it may be wise to limit the amount of time that they will discuss this. For example, the couple can establish a one hour period each day as a free communication time in which the injured partner can ask anything she wants and the husband is compelled to answer honestly and openly. Outside of that time, no discussion of the affair can take place. Couples who have done this report that within a short period of time, they are utilizing only a fraction of the time previously set aside for this discussion. The injured partner is not typically as interested in the specific responses as much as they are in simply knowing that they can ask questions and have some level of confidence that their husband will actually answer them truthfully.

As the couple begins to heal from the infidelity, they can start working on building trust, forgiving themselves and one another; as well as figuring out what went wrong in the relationship. This is a long process and these various tasks or components are accomplished in parallel. I believe the starting point is to stop blaming and to accept the idea that both partners contributed to a situation that led to the affair. It is not about blame as much as it is about making an honest assessment of the marriage and what needs to change to make it work. The affair happened – that can't be changed. The couple can however, take steps to minimize the chances of it happening again. This involves both spouses being willing to examine the relationship and to change things about themselves and the way they interact with one another.

Take the case of Brian and Kathy. Kathy had just been promoted to a supervisory job within the company that she works. This promotion brought in more money, but also caused her to have to work many more hours, including some additional traveling time. As a result, she was not able to give Brian the attention he was used to getting from her. They subsequently began drifting further and further apart until one weekend while Kathy was out of town, Brian ended up sleeping with a woman he met while working out at the gym. The affair continued for a period of about six months. In retrospect, Brian and Kathy believe that the affair was a response to Brian not getting the attention he needed from his wife. He felt that he was not important, that the marriage was not important, that he and the marriage were secondary to her career, and that she was not really there for him.

In Kathy's defense however, Brian never vocalized any of these concerns or feelings to her. They did not have any intimate conversations about their personal feelings and the impact of life situations upon their marriage. They simply responded by withdrawing from the marriage and from each other. Knowing now that the job made Brian feel abandoned, Kathy could do things to make him feel more loved and accepted. He could possibly go with her on some of her trips, they could work at spending more time together, and they could make regular conversation a priority. He could also take steps to do more around the house so that they can spend more time together. He could do things to make her feel more appreciated and supported in both her work and at home. By doing these things, Brian and Kathy could draw closer together instead of drifting apart.

The betraying spouse will likely feel confused by all that has happened. He may feel remorseful and apologetic, but will also likely feel hopeless about the situation and lost as to what to do to make things better or to correct it. He will want to fix it – in the shortest amount of time and with the least amount of effort possible. Confronting the issue and the problems in the marriage is painful. He will be impatient about making it go away and this will come across to the injured partner as him not caring or not being really remorseful about what happened or serious about making it better. She will feel like he isn't really interested in fixing the marriage or changing himself, but rather, pacifying her and trying to convince her to just let everything go.

The injured partner will feel extremely hurt and betrayed. She will even want him to somehow pay for what he has done, to feel humiliated, and to suffer like she has. At the same time, she is seeking comfort and reassurance that somehow, through all the pain and misery, things will be ok – that she will be ok, and that they will be ok. She needs him to say that he is sorry and to somehow explain why he did what he did. The irony is that he probably doesn't know himself. He may also need to forgive himself before he will have the strength, courage, and self-awareness to ask for forgiveness from her. So what does he need to do to forgive himself? The process starts with having a support network that will validate what he is feeling and do so without ripping him apart or blaming him. He needs to accept responsibility, but that will come with time. He is in many ways like an injured child who needs comforting and reassurance. He needs to know that people still love him, that God loves him, and that he is still a good person. He needs to be reminded that people make mistakes and that through these mistakes they can change and be made stronger. Forgiveness is a process that takes time and involves the rebuilding of trust.

I have had many individuals who have cheated on their spouse say to me, "if he (she) would just trust me again." The betraying spouse feels that the injured partner should move on, forget what happened, and put it in the past. Along with this comes the idea that trust should be able to be restored once an apology is made or a verbalized intent to change is made. The reality however, is that most individuals will trust someone up to the point that something happens to take away or destroy the trust. Once this occurs, trust is restored incrementally over time. The key point here is that the betraying spouse will have to be very deliberate in his actions and words so that trust can be re-established. If he says that he is going to do something, he must do it. There can't be any perception of secrecy, deceit, or him doing something that would give his wife reason to doubt his integrity. A good analogy of the trust rebuilding process is the concept of a penny jar. Assume you have a penny jar that is completely full. You see something at the store you want to purchase and in doing so, spend every penny in the jar. You like having a full penny jar so you make the decision to refill the jar. This will require saving and will take time. You put every extra penny you can in the jar, but it takes a while. You find yourself getting impatient and wanting to fill it faster, but you have a limited amount of extra pennies. Finally, after saving every extra penny you can, the jar is full and you realize it took months to accomplish this task. Rebuilding trust after an affair is the same. The jar is empty and every time you do something responsible and trustworthy, with the intent of doing the right thing and making the marriage work, you will build a little more trust. Likewise, if something negative happens, the trust will dissipate again and the process starts over. It may take months and even years to rebuild the trust. If the trust is repeatedly destroyed, the injured partner may even begin to question whether it is worth the effort. It is for these reasons that couples must do all they possibly can to rebuild the trust and be completely honest with one another.

Infidelity is one of the most difficult things a couple can experience. It will likely change the relationship forever – good and bad. As stated earlier, infidelity rarely, if ever, occurs in a vacuum. There are reasons the infidelity occurred. The couple must discover these reasons and correct the associated problems, while also gaining forgiveness and rebuilding trust. This is a process that couples rarely, if ever, can accomplish by themselves. Healing is complex and will likely require professional intervention. Let the process of healing begin. Do not wait another day.

INFIDELITY

Couple Exercise

Instructions: Answer the following questions as completely and honestly as possible. Do not share your answers with your spouse until both of you have finished answering these questions.

1. What, in your opinion constitutes infidelity? If your spouse was asked the same question, how might he or she answer the same question?

_____
_____
_____
_____
_____
_____
_____
_____
_____
_____
_____
_____
_____
_____
_____
_____
_____
_____
_____
_____
_____
_____
_____
_____

2. If an infidelity has occurred, how has it left you feeling? If it hasn't happened, identify what feelings you would likely have both as the one that had the affair and as the injured partner?

_____

_____

_____

_____

_____

_____

_____

_____

_____

_____

_____

_____

_____

_____

_____

_____

_____

_____

_____

_____

_____

_____

_____

_____

_____

_____

_____

_____

_____

_____

_____

_____

_____

_____

_____

_____

_____

_____

_____

_____

3. If an affair has occurred, where have you found hope? If an affair has not occurred, where do you think you would look for and ultimately find hope?

_____
_____
_____
_____
_____
_____
_____
_____
_____
_____
_____
_____
_____
_____
_____
_____
_____
_____
_____
_____
_____
_____
_____
_____
_____
_____
_____
_____
_____
_____
_____
_____
_____
_____
_____
_____

4. If an affair has occurred, where are you in the recovery process and what has contributed to your healing individually and as a couple? If an affair has not occurred, what do you think would be most helpful in trying to heal individually and as a couple?

_____

_____

_____

_____

_____

_____

_____

_____

_____

_____

_____

_____

_____

_____

_____

_____

_____

_____

_____

_____

_____

_____

_____

_____

_____

_____

_____

_____

_____

_____

_____

_____

_____

_____

_____

5. Do you know people (past or present) that have had affairs Y // N? If so describe the impact this has had on you and your understanding of affairs and relationships.

_____
_____
_____
_____
_____
_____
_____
_____
_____
_____
_____
_____
_____
_____
_____
_____
_____
_____
_____
_____
_____
_____
_____
_____
_____
_____
_____
_____
_____
_____
_____
_____
_____
_____
_____

6. If an affair has occurred, what have you identified as contributors to it (individually and relationally)? What have you done to change or correct these things? If an affair has not occurred, what can you identify now (individually or relationally) as potential problems or red flags as contributors to an affair? What have you done or can you do to change or fix these things?

_____

_____

_____

_____

_____

_____

_____

_____

_____

_____

_____

_____

_____

_____

_____

_____

_____

_____

_____

_____

_____

_____

_____

_____

_____

_____

_____

_____

_____

_____

_____

_____

_____

_____

_____

_____

_____

_____

_____

7. If your spouse was to have an affair, who would you tell and why? Who would you consider your sources of support (rank in order of preference if possible)? Who would specifically not tell and why?

_____
_____
_____
_____
_____
_____
_____
_____
_____
_____
_____
_____
_____
_____
_____
_____
_____
_____
_____
_____
_____
_____
_____
_____
_____
_____
_____
_____
_____
_____
_____
_____
_____
_____
_____
_____

Now that you have answered these questions, sit down with your spouse and discuss each of these questions and how you answered them. Pay particular attention to needs, feelings, and messages that are developed through the discussion.

<u>Action Plan</u>: As a couple, we have decided to make the following changes or to start doing the following things with regards to infidelity: We will sit down and discuss our progress on this plan in 4 weeks.

(Date and time of next meeting) _____

_____
_____
_____
_____
_____
_____
_____
_____
_____
_____
_____
_____
_____
_____
_____
_____
_____
_____
_____
_____
_____
_____
_____
_____
_____
_____
_____
_____
_____
_____
_____
_____

CHAPTER SIX

Parenting

Decisions Regarding Family Planning

As discussed in a previous chapter, the decision to have children and how many children to have must be made by the couple - together. It is not unusual for couples to disagree about these things, having previously assumed that their spouse or partner wanted the same things they do. The problem is that these couples have not discussed these issues and are therefore grounded in fantasy as opposed to reality. Couples must come together and discuss the issue of when to have children and how many to have. In other words, it is all about timing and quantity. These two decisions are foundational to future decisions involving career, schooling, family roles and responsibilities, and financial wellness. It is important to note that even the best family planning efforts sometimes fail. In my opinion, children are a gift from God and His plans and our plans do not always coincide. We simply need to do the best we can and leave the rest to Him.

Why do couples fail to have these discussions early in their relationship? I believe that individuals are afraid of being perceived as "moving too fast" in the relationship or that they are afraid there will be a disagreement – one that could ultimately end the relationship. They may consciously or even subconsciously feel that they are better off waiting to discuss these critical issues until they have been married a little while, after the relationship has matured some, and there is likely to be a deeper level of commitment. I don't think this is difficult to understand or even agree with. The problem, however, is that couples can, and often are, blindsided by the opinions and desires of their spouse on these issues when they do finally come up in conversation. In extreme cases, these differences can destroy the marriage. What I am saying is that couples need to communicate – to have these important discussions at the appropriate time and make the best decisions possible.

Being Involved

I am of the opinion that the two most important ingredients for being a good parent are to love your children and to be involved in their lives. For most of us, the love comes naturally. We are totally blown away by their beauty, sweetness, and innocence from the second they come into this world. They are easy to love because they offer so much love in return – unconditional love that is given to us despite our faults and imperfections. The difficult part is being involved in their lives. When they are infants, most of the care-giving in traditional families is given by the mother. This may cause the father to withdraw, isolate, and even feel neglected or feel that he doesn't have an important role. Fortunately, times are changing and fathers are becoming much more involved in the lives of their infant children. They are helping with the feeding, changing the diapers, and getting up in the middle of the night. They are also spending more time with the infant children playing and socializing. This is a great and wonderful thing. I wish I had done more as a young father at this juncture in my children's lives. If you are a father of a young infant child and are not involved in their care - start now. It will change your life and the life of your child.

As children begin to grow, fathers typically become more involved. The children require less attention and are able to do more things. It is important that both parents spend time with the children individually and that they do things together as a family. It is about spending quality time together. When I was growing up, my family spent a lot of time camping in the Southern California desert, riding motorcycles and ATVs. This brought our family much closer together and gave us a lot of memories that I still carry with me today. When I was a child, my father also took my brother and I target shooting in the hills near Hemet. This was a great time as it gave us quality time with our Dad and usually our uncle as well.

My father worked as a service manager at a Ford truck dealership and would sometimes take me to work with him when I had a day off school. This was a treat as it gave me the opportunity to watch my Dad work, interacting with customers, as well as his mechanics. The best part however, was being able to go to lunch with my Dad – just the two of us. My father had me later in life – when he was 51 years old. What was really great however was that he did what we did, even in his sixties and seventies. He coached our little league teams and taught my brother and I how to play baseball, how to follow rules, and most importantly, how to be a good sport and have fun. He led by example and he was involved in our lives.

My parenting experience has been somewhat different. I have been in the Navy for the last 27 years, having enlisted at least a year before I met my wife. I have missed anniversaries, birthdays, holidays, and a host of other events. I have not coached little league and sometimes struggle just to make it to the games. My wife has sometimes had to fill in as the father, grabbing a glove or a football so that my son (and daughters) had someone to play catch with. The point here is that we don't live in an ideal world and we must simply put forth our best effort and do the best we possibly can. Children feel loved when people spend time with them doing things that they enjoy doing. I love jogging with my seventeen year-old daughter. It is our time together. I also enjoy watching movies or playing games with my children. I do not like games so this is not easy for me and my kids recognize this. I try to do it anyways because I want them to know that I love and care about them. I also try to have a daddy-daughter date night on a somewhat regular basis with my three daughters. My youngest daughter, Kimberly, used to get dressed up in her nicest dress, have her mother or older sisters do her hair – just so she and I could go to McDonalds (her choice not mine) on a date with her dad. The dates have become more expensive over the years as a dinner at McDonalds has changed to a dinner Olive Garden. Dates don't have to cost money however, to be fun. An evening at the beach, playing Frisbee in the park, or window shopping at the mall could be just as good. The point I am trying to make is that we need to spend time with our children – individually and collectively. As my two oldest daughters are now in college, I realize how much I have missed and how much I would change if I could. I just pray that they know how much I love them – whether I was there or not.

As children get older, they start spending more time with their friends and less time with the family. This is simply part of growing up. As parents, we need to try not to compete with our children's friends for their time. We need to carve out time and plan ahead to do things together. For example, my kids know that we are going to church on Sunday morning. We oftentimes take two cars because my son likes to ride with me in the pick-up truck and go get sodas together after church. It has become a ritual and a great time for us to talk and to bond. I once heard a man say that a father should never go anywhere without taking at least one of his children. With every drive comes an opportunity for conversation and subsequently, an opportunity to build relationships. When my son and I return home from our soda outing, he quickly changes and within minutes is usually out the door on his way to his friend's house to play. When I was a child, my dad used to take me in his truck to visit a horse that we had named Whitey. I eventually outgrew these weekly treks, but I fondly remember them now and love my dad for it. Little things can and do make a big difference. We never know what memories we are creating.

Structure and Discipline

We see much debate in the media on the issue of children and structure in the home. How much structure do kids need? How much is too much and how much is not enough? Many parents think they need to be dictators and authoritarians while others believe they need to be friends with their children. I believe that the most effective parents are somewhere in the middle. Children need to know that there are rules and standards, and that there will be consequences for subsequent violations. In the Navy I have had Commanding Officers who have stated that each and every Sailor will be treated with dignity and respect, regardless of their rank or position. Similarly, parents are in charge of the home and the family, but the children still need to be treated with dignity and respect. If they break the rules, they should be held accountable and punished accordingly, but with dignity and respect. The problem is that we sometimes speak and act before our brain has time to engage and the tongue can do significant harm to another person – we must control our emotions and be careful in what we say and do.

When it comes to structure and discipline, it is important that we, as parents, clearly communicate to our children the rules that they are expected to follow. There should be no confusion or doubt in their minds as to what is expected of them with regards to their behavior. Once these expectations are communicated, they need to be enforced – by both parents. Children will often try to manipulate their parents, going to the softer or more lenient parent, or sometimes asking one parent and then the other. Many of us grew up not really fearing the spanking that mom would oftentimes give, but we sure feared dad and what he would do. I can count the spankings I received from my father on one hand (barely), but I remember each one as though it was yesterday. They left an impression to say the least. Many of us grew up hearing those famous words, "just wait until your father gets home." Discipline needs to be effectively used by both parents and should be used to teach, to punish, and to deter.

We need to discipline our children in a fair and consistent manner. Punishment should be age appropriate, fair for the given offense, and consistent from child to child. For example, if little Johnny gets three days restriction for talking back to his mother, his sister should probably get a similar punishment for the same offense. I am also personally in favor of spanking a child when necessary to get their attention. It needs to be done with an open hand however and should not leave a mark on the child. My experience has been that this isn't needed very often, is more effective with boys, and is typically most effective at a younger age (approximately 4-8). Time out is also very effective at a younger age, but as they get older, the most effective punishment seems to be removal of desired privileges. This could be television, videogames, cell phone, computer etc.

When I was about twelve, I got in trouble for throwing rocks at passing cars as they drove by on a street near our house. I would like to say that my brother instigated the whole thing, but that probably wasn't the case. One of these drivers stopped suddenly after the rock went crashing into his passenger side door. He jumped out of the car, came running towards us and even though we were well covered, he eventually found us hiding in the bushes. He then took us to our house where my dad took over responsibility for dishing out punishment. I still remember what he did. We were supposed to go motorcycle riding the next day and he simply told us that we were no longer going and that we would do chores and yard work instead. The punishment was effective. What was equally effective however was seeing the disappointment on my father's face as he learned of what we had been doing. If you want to effectively punish a teenager, take away their cell phone or driving privileges if they are older. They would prefer for you to have removed a kidney or a lung.

When disciplining children, parents need to be on the same page so that the children see a united front. Even if both parents don't completely agree with each other, they must support one another and act accordingly in front of the children. They also need to communicate to the children that they are still loved. This equates to "hating the sin, but loving the sinner." This is where respect and dignity come strongly into play. I have found that I get really good results when I take the time to sit down with my children, have a good discussion about what they did and why it was wrong, and perhaps most importantly, reaffirm my love for them as my children and as people of value and worth. I also think it is good when disciplining children to demonstrate mercy and grace by giving them "time off for good behavior" or a commuted sentence (perhaps with a probation time attached). This can't be done every time however, as they will come to expect it.

When one considers the term *structure*, the word *routine* or *schedule* may come to mind. It is important for children to have a routine and to learn how to manage it. In other words, children need to have a reasonable wake-up time and associated morning routine, just as they need to have a reasonable bedtime and nightly routine. They need sleep to function properly and they need to eat regular healthy meals; as well as having time for exercise, play, and homework as appropriate for their age. I feel that the key for success with regard to structure predictability and balance. Parents that let kids stay up late or sleep in until afternoon hours on the weekend are doing them a disservice. Our bodies thrive on structure. Children in particular, need that structure embedded into their daily lives.

Trust and Responsibility

As children mature, they need to be given additional opportunities for increased responsibility. When a child is really young, we get excited as parents when they simply pick-up their toys. As they get older, we expect them to keep their rooms clean (usually not an expectation that is fulfilled), as well as helping out with chores around the house and in the yard. We need to communicate to them that we trust them; that we believe in them; that they are competent and capable; and that we are there for guidance and support when necessary.

We need to encourage them and give them room to explore and grow. Like a small child, we sometimes need to let children of all ages fall. Like us, they will learn from their mistakes (hopefully). Many parents are over-protective and fail to let their children "skin a knee." They can't learn from their experiences if we do this. There are also parents who fail to protect their children and instead of "skinning a knee," they "break their neck." We must provide adequate levels of protection, supervision, and guidance. We must teach our children in such a way that when they must do it alone, they will be ready.

Special Considerations for Blended Families

Many people in America today are in what is referred to as a blended family. This simply means that they have children from previous relationships or marriages. Why is this significant? Being part of a family can be challenging and difficult, but being part of several families simultaneously can be complex, chaotic, and even overwhelming. Think about it this way – instead of having a parent and children (single-parent family) or even two parents and children (traditional nuclear family), blended families typically consist of a married couple who likely both have children in the home (part of full time) from previous relationships. They may also have their own biological children living at home as well. Connected to these children from previous relationships are usually ex-wives and/or husbands who may have shared custody of the children, as well as new spouses who will ultimately share in some of the very complicated parenting responsibilities. Considering the structure of these families, it is no wonder why things get emotional and tense. Given the nature and dynamics associated with such a complex environment, things are bound to be difficult.

The most important elements necessary for success in the blended family environment are flexibility and communication. The parents, step-parents, children, and step-children need to communicate in a way that they all understand what is going on and what is expected of them. This sounds a lot easier than it actually is. Couples split oftentimes on bad terms and trying to get them to communicate with each other, yet alone work together and compromise, can seem almost impossible. Yet, this is precisely what is needed. They must put aside their feelings and work collaboratively with one another for the sake of the children. The children are not pawns to be used by the parents as leverage. They are not spies and they are not material possessions. The sooner couples realize this, the better things will be – for them, for the family system, and most importantly, for the children.

Discipline is a particularly sensitive issue in blended families because the question of who is the parent and who has earned the right to discipline the children are raised. Children oftentimes do not recognize step-parents as having parental rights and privileges, and therefore, will not sustain any effort by these individuals to provide discipline. Ground rules need to be established early on with regards to the authority, rights, privileges, and associated boundaries of each parent or adult involved. I was not raised in a blended family, but through the process of counseling many blended families, I strongly feel that step-parents need to be able to discipline all of the children when necessary, especially if the biological parent is unavailable. Step-parents are adults in the home and they need to be given the respect and authority to make parental decisions and discipline the children as appropriate. Like any other couple however, these couples need to discuss the issue of discipline at length so that they can be on the same page with regards to expectations concerning rules that need to be enforced and appropriate consequences when these rules are violated. All parents need to have this conversation so that parents come across as consistent and fair. Children need to know that any parent in the home has the right to discipline them when house rules are broken. There should be no confusion on this issue.

The issue of discipline becomes even more confusing and more difficult to manage when the children are visiting the other biological parent and his or her spouse (the other step-parent). It is challenging to be consistent between parents in the same home when it comes to disciplining the children. It is virtually impossible when considering two couples, four different people in two separate locations. Parents in these homes must sit down together and negotiate expectations, rules, consequences, and procedures for disciplining the children under these conditions. There is more than one right answer. The issue isn't as much how it is done, as much as it is about consistency. If the parents come together and actually develop a policy and a plan, they will be modeling communication, teamwork, and respect. They will also be showing the children that they are all on the same page with regards to discipline and that they will not be manipulated or taken advantage of.

Children in blended families will often say things like "mom (dad) lets me do it." The bottom line is that the parents in each individual household are free to set whatever rules they wish (within reason of course). Although it would be nice if both households had the exact same rules, we don't live in an ideal world so that isn't very likely. The children must understand that there will be some differences (hopefully minimal ones) and that they still need to abide by the rules in the home that they are in. When differences are present however, parents should communicate with one another and see if there is room for compromise or collaboration on the issue. It seems that in most cases, common ground could be reached. It seems that the solution to blended family issues is really communication – between the parents themselves (all sets) and between the parents and the children. There should be absolute clarity with regards to expectations and consequences. Having a child say "I didn't know" is not acceptable and will lead to problems stemming from a breakdown in discipline and structure.

PARENTING

Couple Exercise

Instructions: Answer the following questions as completely and honestly as possible. Do not share your answers with your spouse until both of you have finished answering these questions.

1. Describe the conversations you and your spouse have had regarding family planning (having children) thus far. How many children do you want? How many children does your spouse want? How soon does each of you want children? If there are differences on these issues, what have you done to resolve them? How have these differences and resultant discussions made you feel?

_____

_____

_____

_____

_____

_____

_____

_____

_____

_____

_____

_____

_____

_____

_____

_____

_____

_____

_____

_____

2. What are the positive and negative things you learned growing up with regards to being a good parent? Which of these do you want to emulate and which do you want to avoid?

_____

_____

_____

_____

_____

_____

_____

_____

_____

_____

_____

_____

_____

_____

_____

_____

_____

_____

_____

_____

_____

_____

_____

_____

_____

_____

_____

_____

_____

_____

_____

_____

_____

_____

_____

3. Rate yourself as a parent (if applicable) on a scale from 0-10 with 10 being highest_____ Why did you rate yourself at this level? What do you consider your strengths and weaknesses as a parent? What would you like to change?

_____
_____
_____
_____
_____
_____
_____
_____
_____
_____
_____
_____
_____
_____
_____
_____
_____
_____
_____
_____
_____
_____
_____
_____
_____
_____
_____
_____
_____
_____
_____
_____
_____
_____
_____
_____
_____

4. Describe your idea of the ideal parent – the mother or father you want to be – now or in the future.

_____

_____

_____

_____

_____

_____

_____

_____

_____

_____

_____

_____

_____

_____

_____

_____

_____

_____

_____

_____

_____

_____

_____

_____

_____

_____

_____

_____

_____

_____

_____

_____

_____

5. Describe your beliefs about disciplining children. Give examples of the types of discipline that are acceptable and the types of offenses they might be used for. Explain how you and your spouse agree and/or disagree with regards to discipline.

6. Describe the role of structure and routine in your home with regards to the children. If you don't currently have children, try to imagine having children and describe what structure and routine might look like in their daily lives. What routines and rituals do you feel are most important and why?

_____
_____
_____
_____
_____
_____
_____
_____
_____
_____
_____
_____
_____
_____
_____
_____
_____
_____
_____
_____
_____
_____
_____
_____
_____
_____
_____
_____
_____
_____
_____
_____
_____
_____

7. How would you develop trust and responsibility in your children? Be specific in your responses. How did your parents or caregivers show you that they trusted you and how were you taught responsibility?

_____

_____

_____

_____

_____

_____

_____

_____

_____

_____

_____

_____

_____

_____

_____

_____

_____

_____

_____

_____

_____

_____

_____

_____

_____

_____

_____

_____

_____

_____

_____

_____

_____

_____

_____

_____

_____

_____

_____

_____

8. Describe how you are currently involved in your children's lives? How does your current level of involvement make you feel? What would you like to change and why? Do you feel that your spouse is satisfied with your current level of involvement? Why or why not?

_____
_____
_____
_____
_____
_____
_____
_____
_____
_____
_____
_____
_____
_____
_____
_____
_____
_____
_____
_____
_____
_____
_____
_____
_____
_____
_____
_____
_____
_____
_____
_____
_____

Now that you have answered these questions, sit down with your spouse and discuss each of these questions and how you answered them. Pay particular attention to needs, feelings, and messages that are developed through the discussion.

<u>Action Plan</u>: As a couple, we have decided to make the following changes or to start doing the following things with regards to parenting: We will sit down and discuss our progress on this plan in 4 weeks.

(Date and time of next meeting) _____

_____

_____

_____

_____

_____

_____

_____

_____

_____

_____

_____

_____

_____

_____

_____

_____

_____

_____

_____

_____

_____

_____

_____

_____

_____

_____

_____

_____

_____

CHAPTER SEVEN

Grief & Loss

Grief and Loss

Losing a loved one can be one of the hardest, most difficult, and challenging experiences an individual will ever face. This experience, however, may be even more difficult from the standpoint of the couple or the family relationship. In this chapter, I will discuss the impact of losing a parent, a child, and a spouse on the couple relationship. I will also identify resources and tools that can be employed for helping couples through the grieving process. I would like to begin by simply saying that the process of grieving is a very personal one. There is no specific right or wrong way to grieve and there is no predetermined right amount of time that the process should take. I hear people say "It has been eight months now. It is time to get over it and move on with your life." This statement is insensitive and although the individual likely means no harm, it invalidates the person's feelings regarding the loss. The communicated message may be interpreted as "you are being weak. The person is dead and acting this way is not doing anyone any good." In the end, statements such as this do nobody any good.

Death of a Parent

We all know that someday our parents, like everyone else, are going to die; but that knowledge alone does not make the experience any easier. I have had the personal experience of losing both of my parents and have counseled numerous individuals regarding the loss of a parent in my job as a Navy Chaplain and as a therapist. It is never an easy situation – nor should it be. The overwhelming nature of the situation can seem almost unbearable at times. It is important to note however, that the rollercoaster of emotions that are experienced during the grieving process are both expected and normal given what is happening.

My mother had been ill for a number of years prior to her death. It was hard watching her deteriorate and when she did finally die, I felt a significant loss; but I also felt a sense of relief for her in that she would not suffer any longer. I am ashamed to admit that this sense of relief may even have spilled over onto me as I probably felt relief in not having to watch her deteriorate any longer as well. My mother was seventy-five years old at the time of her death and she died from complications from emphysema due to years of smoking. I did not view her as old and I feel that she could have lived a much longer life had it not been for the health issues. Feeling that way has probably made the grief just a little bit harder.

My father, on the other hand, was almost ninety-seven years old when he died. He had been in relatively great health until about three months prior to his death. He drove up until the time he got sick and worked at least part-time until he was ninety. He died from complications brought about by pneumonia. He deteriorated rather rapidly during the three months that he became sick and was on hospice care during much of that time as well. My brother and I were able to take on some of the caretaking responsibilities during the final weeks. This was good from the perspective of being able to be there and spend time together, but difficult from the standpoint of not wanting to remember him in that condition. I really wanted to remember him the way I did as a kid – working, playing, and having fun together. Thankfully, I still have many of those fond memories to hang on to. In both cases, I was present when my parents died. Being there helped, but it is important to note that these were very different experiences physically, emotionally, and spiritually. Please realize that no two experiences involving death will be exactly the same. There may be similarities, but there will be many differences as well.

When a parent gets ill there are a lot of financial and logistical issues to consider. This was covered to some extent in the chapter on finances. It is critical that all applicable family members get together and discuss responsibilities and efforts to be taken to care for the individual prior to their death, as well as estate issues following the death. This may sound disrespectful or even morbid, but it is the reality of the situation. Some of the issues that must be faced are financial; others are medical; and some legal. This is why proper estate planning is so important. These discussions also raise questions about life insurance, long-term care insurance, and even funeral and burial arrangements. I do not suggest waiting until the person dies to start discussing and even planning. Having to make these types of decisions during a time of mourning makes things just that much harder. Families going through situations such as this should contact their attorney, insurance agent, financial advisor, and funeral home as appropriate as soon as possible.

One of the scenarios to consider when caring for elderly or ill parents is a dynamic that some have referred to as the sandwich generation. This is the situation that occurs when a couple has to take care of their parents while at the same time raising their own children. This leaves them stuck in the middle – like a sandwich. The physical, financial, and emotional demands of a situation such as this can be overwhelming. Consider this, you and your spouse both work and have two young school-age children at home. Your mother develops dementia and you decide to have her move in with you. As a result, you determine that either you do not have access to professional in-home care (due to insurance, cost etc.) so you quit your job in order to remain home and provide the necessary care. Your budget was developed based on two incomes so you now have a financial deficit each month due to spending more than you make. Situations such as this one are not uncommon, but very few people adequately plan for them.

Consider your current retirement planning. Have you taken into consideration having to care for an elderly or ill parent? Have you taken into consideration the possibility of one or more of your children returning home to live with you due to problems with work, relationships, and/or school? In today's economy, many good, highly-educated, and hard-working people are finding themselves unemployed. Are you prepared for events such as these? We need to start considering these situations in our long-term plans. You may be within sight of retirement, only to have all your plans of living on the beach or golf course shot out from under you due to the unexpected illness of a parent.

So enough doom and gloom, let's examine the situation more closely and look at what we can do about it – things that will resolve it or that will at least minimize the severity. As stated previously, planning is critical. It is important for the children (and spouses as applicable) to know the wishes of their parents with regards to end-of-life issues, funeral services, burial etc. The individual should get a will or trust if they don't already have one. They should also identify all important papers and put them in a protected, yet known location. I heard about an individual that created an instruction booklet for his family prior to his death. It was a step-by-step guide to taking care of everything that would need to be accomplished following his death. Detailed planning such as this lessens the burden considerably for those that must dispose of the estate. Conversations such as this may be difficult, but they are necessary. It is important for all applicable parties to know in advance what is expected of them both prior to (especially if long-term care is required), and following the death.

When I was younger, my maternal grandmother reached a point in her life where she required additional care. She lived in Texas. My aunt (the oldest of three daughters) also lived in Texas and provided the actual physical assistance and care. My impression was that this was a significant sacrifice for her and involved physical, emotional, and perhaps even spiritual costs. My mother and other aunt both lived in California. Although they probably would have liked to help more, they were simply too far away and were not in a position to do so. They may have helped financially or in other ways, but not in the same manner as their older sister. From my experience counseling couples and families, this is not an uncommon situation. One child will oftentimes take on the caretaking role – and most of the burden in the process. This may be because they are closer, have more money, or because they do not work outside the home. Situations such as this can result in feelings of animosity, resentment, and bitterness. It can wreck havoc on the family and their relationships. This is why families must sit down in advance and work out a plan that is fair and equitable. Don't wait until you need to respond – plan now.

Death of a Child

There is a popular saying that "no parent should outlive their children." I agree with this statement. As a Chaplain at a hospital, I had to face this situation on numerous occasions. I recall one case, in particular, that involved the drowning death of a little boy – a boy that reminded me of my own son. I spent several hours with the couple in the emergency room as the doctors tried fervently to save this young child's life; continuing through the point that the doctor informed the parents that their life-saving efforts had failed; all the way until and even beyond the point at which they left for home – a home that had become hollow by their loss. I was with them in the emergency room for 4-5 hours while they were at the hospital, and I talked with them several more times later by phone and in person. The pain that this couple felt was almost indescribable. That was almost five years ago. Today, they are still together enjoying their life together as they raise their other children. They will always have a void in their lives and in their family, but they are pressing forward, persevering and enduring – something many in similar situations are unable or unwilling to do. When they left the hospital however,

I remember going to my office shutting the door, and crying. I was touched forever by that event and the resultant mark of loss that touched my heart. I also remember calling my wife, telling her what had happened and asking her to hug each of our four children for me. I then hung up the phone, wiped my eyes, and continued my day of visiting patients and counseling those that came to see me.

People have asked me why children die. That is a difficult question and I am not sure I have a good answer. I have prayed about it however, and this is the answer that God has given me or inspired me with. Let me state, in case it isn't obvious; I am a Christian and the following statements are presented from that perspective. I personally believe that we are all children of a loving God and are created in his image. I also believe that we all have a purpose here on earth. Perhaps we die and return to heaven when our purpose or mission is complete. That is probably the case, but I do not know that for certain. I feel that children that die at a young age are particularly special in God's eyes and that they are taken home because they have a more pressing mission or job there with Him. That does not mean however, that God does not care about the rest of His children, particularly the family and friends of the young child. I don't think that it is a casual decision or event. God knows the impact and He knows how it will affect others. He is the one with the ultimate plan and He is the one with the facts to make the tough decisions. I have faith in Him, His love, and in His plan. I also believe that we will see one another in Heaven. Children do not have to accept Christ to be saved if they die at an age before they can fully comprehend the true meaning and significance of such a decision. The same is not true for adults however. We must accept Christ or we will not be saved and will not go to Heaven. If you have not made that decision yet, I implore you to contact any Christian church or pastor, Christian neighbor or coworker and make a profession of faith in which you accept Jesus Christ as your Lord and Savior. It may be too late in an hour, a day, a week, or a month. Please – stop reading and do it now. It is by the grace and atoning blood of Christ that we all have the opportunity to be saved. These beliefs give me hope and these are the primary things I would rely on if I was too loose one of my children. I hope that they can give you hope as well.

Years ago, I had just reported to a Marine combat battalion as the Chaplain. A young Staff Non-Commissioned Officer had just lost his son to a prolonged illness. The child was about four or five years old. I attended the funeral at the request of the family. It was one of the most touching services I have ever attended. What made it so special was that they were not simply mourning his death; they were celebrating his life – regardless of how short it actually was. The child loved country music so the service consisted of several of his favorite songs. There were tears of sadness and laughs of joy as stories were told and funny events recalled. At the end of the service, everyone in attendance was given a balloon and we proceeded to the parking lot where all of these colorful balloons were let go, ascending in mass toward the sky in what could only be described as both magnificent and beautiful. This service was not only a celebration of a life, but it was also an opportunity for closure for those that had the blessing of having known this young child. Events such as this are important when losing someone close – particularly a child. It may be difficult in the moment, but it is part of a healing process – a journey if you will.

In addition to a funeral service, there are other things that can be helpful in the healing process. I like to encourage parents and loved ones to create something in honor of and in memory of the individual. Examples include planting gardens, trees, or flowers; building a club house for other children to use; naming a boat after the child; dedicating a baseball, football or other sporting facility after them;

establishing a scholarship, charity, or foundation in their name. Regardless of what is chosen, the goal is to make it meaningful to those that knew the child – something that takes into consideration the personality, interests, and character of the child.

Another very useful thing that friends and family members can do to aid in the healing process is to dedicate an event or accomplishment to the child. For example, an individual or family could run a 5k, 10k, half, or full marathon in honor of the person – dedicating their effort and any results to the child. When I was a Chaplain at Navy boot camp in Great Lakes, Illinois, I had several recruits dedicate milestone events such as final physical fitness tests, battle stations (a culminating final training event), and even graduation itself to a sibling or other close relative that died while the person was at boot camp. This was very helpful to these recruits who, because of the environment and associated demands, had very few options for expressing grief and dealing with the accompanying emotions.

One of the biggest issues for parents who lose a child is that of forgiveness. They blame themselves, each other, and even their other children for their child's death. This is not healthy and will not help anyone. Even if someone did something that contributed to or facilitated the death, it was likely not intentional. This is extremely important as accidents happen and people do make mistakes – even big ones. I am not saying this will be easy, I am just saying that in times like this, families need to turn towards one another in love and in support. Blaming each other or even oneself will severely impede the healing process – a process that needs to take place if they are ever going to recover, yet alone experience the full joy of life that God intends for all of us to have. Forgiveness, in my opinion, begins with the recognition that nobody is perfect and we need to let others and ourselves off the hook. That does not mean however, that we can't learn from the experience and do things better or differently in the future. Similarly, forgiveness does not mean that we forget about the child and all that he or she meant to us.

There is also a spiritual piece that involves knowing that God has a plan and that regardless of what we do or don't do, certain outcomes are essentially inevitable. Does that mean that the person would have died anyways or that they would be alive if the events had not occurred as they did? I don't know – and either do you. Stop second guessing yourself. It isn't going to help. We need to have faith however, in God and in all that He is as creator and sustainer of the world. This is part of His plan. Trust in it and in Him and things will eventually get better. Turn to those you care about and love the most and seek the support you need. Love and hug one another. You should also stay busy physically and socially in activities and with people that you enjoy. Do the things that give your life meaning. Rediscover and seek after your passions. You must find balance in your life and stay busy doing things that give you a sense of purpose. As mentioned earlier, there is no right way or wrong way of doing things – as long as it doesn't harm you or others. Grieving takes time – and that amount of time is not a fixed quantity. Some people simply take longer than others and that doesn't make it wrong. It is also important to see out professional counseling individually and as a couple. Go to someone that has experience and training in grief counseling. Contact you pastor, Priest, Rabbi, or Imam for assistance as well.

Death of a Spouse

When I think of what it would be like to lose my wife - my best friend, a river of emotion flows over me. I would be so lonely without her and I would feel so lost as a result. We look forward to a long life together, and perhaps we take that for granted. Nobody really knows how long they or someone they love has left in this world. We simply hope, and sometimes assume, that it will be a long time. That may not, however, be the case.

When a spouse dies, I believe the first thing to do is to allow the grieving process to occur. Well-intentioned friends and family members are going to bombard you with visits, phone calls, emails, text messages, cards, and perhaps letters in an effort to show you that they care and are worried about you. As a result, you will become very frustrated and will get tired of hearing questions and comments such as "How are you holding up?", "Are you doing okay?", and "it must be a really difficult time." Keep reminding yourself that these individuals really do care – they just aren't being incredibly helpful in the process. The important point is that they do care and for the most part, they are there if you need them. You will want to establish boundaries however and help these individuals better understand the ways that they possibly can be of assistance. It may be necessary to take a vacation and simply get away for awhile. Do what works for you and don't worry what other people think about it. Avoid isolating yourself at home, with the memories. Get out and about, do things that you enjoy and seek out friends and family that you feel comfortable with.

Another question that people sometimes ask when a spouse dies is "when is the right time to box up or get rid of belongings?" I think you will know. I would not do it the next day, but I wouldn't wait years either. There will come a time when you will be able to go through his or her things, boxing up some items, giving some to friends and family, and keeping some for yourself. Perhaps you will want to first decide what you want to keep and put those things away in a secure place. Then select items that are particularly meaningful for others that were close to the individual (based on your experiences and knowledge of the person) and give those away as applicable. Then invite people to come and take anything they would like to have. Take the rest and either give it away or sell it. This process should not take an overly long time and should not prove too difficult to accomplish. This will, however, be an important step in moving forward.

Another important and extremely critical element in dealing with the death of a spouse is discovering their individual identity apart from the spouse. This may sound a little strange, but it is possible that his or her identity is tied so closely to that of the spouse as a couple that he or she doesn't really know who they are individually. They need to learn to find comfort in being alone or with other people. They will need to discover new hobbies and interests, or possibly just get involved again with old ones. One doesn't have to be completely alone however and even a person who lives alone does not have to feel lonely. Pets can also be a great source of comfort and companionship. A dog or cat can be very helpful and extremely therapeutic. I would encourage people who have lost a spouse to go on vacations – either alone or with someone they care about and enjoy spending time with. It is a great opportunity to plan an overdue fishing or hunting trip, or possibly a trip to a national park, Las Vegas, the beaches of Hawaii, or the coast. It may also be a great time to rekindle some relationships – with friends, siblings, or even children. The point is that before you can fully enjoy these relationships and activities, you have to feel good about yourself as an individual again. This takes time and will be a work in progress.

One final issue we need to discuss pertaining to the death of a spouse is if and when to remarry. My wife says that if I die she will not remarry. I think she figured out that I am too much work and doesn't want to go through that again. I have jokingly told her that if she dies, I will wait at least a week, but not much longer than that before remarrying because I am a rotten cook and I enjoy sex far too much to be alone. She didn't laugh.

Although we may joke some about this very serious topic, it is a big question and one worth considering. When is the right time to start dating? I feel that is a personal decision. Now, I would say that if you bring a date to the funeral, people are not going to be impressed. On the other hand, if you meet someone a few months or even years following the death of your spouse, then dating may be completely appropriate. I have heard many people say that you should wait at least a year. That sounds like pretty good advice and a decent rule of thumb, but in the end, it is just a guide. If someone special comes into your life 3-4 months following the death of your husband or wife then who can really say that it isn't a good thing and that you shouldn't date? The important consideration is your emotional state. In other words, are you so lonely or vulnerable that you would attach yourself to the person in an unhealthy way? Similarly, are you so tired of being alone that you would propose to or agree to marry the first person you meet or go out with? It goes without saying that this would be problematic. You don't want to date just because you are lonely or when you are in what some refer to as a rebound position. It isn't fair to you or the other person. As stated earlier, discover who you are again and after you do that, then feel free to find a person you enjoy being around; a person that you think you would enjoy dating, and perhaps even marrying one day.

When you do start dating again, plan on stirring up some significant emotions within the family – especially among adult children. They may think you are too old to start dating again. They may see the other person as not good enough, simply after your money, or trying to replace their deceased mother or father. They aren't going to want to hear that you are lonely. After all, isn't that the purpose of the local senior citizens center? They definitely aren't going to want to hear about your sexual needs or want to see you being affectionate with someone else in public. They may believe that your sexual behavior stopped with the birth of the children. There are some who will want to believe that parents don't have sex at all – at least not when they are older – like age forty. Some people are going to try to keep you from dating and especially marrying, while others, particularly friends, are going to try to set you up. Be careful, many of these people you may go on dates with come with a lot of baggage. You may need a u-haul trailer to carry it all.

Taking into consideration all that we have talked about regarding grief and loss, I hope that you will consider the following points:

1. Grief is a process that takes time. It may follow a fairly common pattern or it may not. It is an individual journey and that journey should be respected. Allow it to simply happen.
2. Death is hard on all concerned. It gets easier over time however -especially with the support of friends, family, and God.
3. Personal resiliency is a key attribute and can be developed and strengthened by finding balance in life – enjoying relationships, hobbies, and work.
4. It is important to find pleasure, meaning, and purpose in all that we do - professionally and personally.

5. It is much easier to grieve when you can find strength from a higher power. Turn to your spiritual self and discover God's presence in the midst of the pain.

6. Allow yourself to feel. Don't be surprised by your emotions and don't let people tell you what or how you should feel.

7. Look for things that work for you. Do more of those things and remember - it is a journey of growth and healing.

GRIEF AND LOSS

Couple Exercise

Instructions: Answer the following questions as completely and honestly as possible. Do not share your answers with your spouse until both of you have finished answering these questions.

1. What did you learn about death and dying growing up? Describe your perceptions of how the grieving process should look. Is it different for men and women - why or why not?

_____
_____
_____
_____
_____
_____
_____
_____
_____
_____
_____
_____
_____
_____
_____
_____
_____
_____
_____
_____
_____
_____
_____
_____
_____

2. Who close to you has died in your life? What was that like for you? What feelings do you remember having? What do you feel now? What has been helpful with respect to the whole grieving process?

_____

_____

_____

_____

_____

_____

_____

_____

_____

_____

_____

_____

_____

_____

_____

_____

_____

_____

_____

_____

_____

_____

_____

_____

_____

_____

_____

_____

_____

_____

_____

_____

_____

3. How do you think the grieving process is different when it involves an adult as opposed to a child?

_____

_____

_____

_____

_____

_____

_____

_____

_____

_____

_____

_____

_____

_____

_____

_____

_____

_____

_____

_____

_____

_____

_____

_____

_____

_____

_____

_____

_____

_____

_____

_____

_____

_____

_____

_____

_____

_____

_____

4. If yours or your spouse's parents are still alive, what end-of life decisions have or still need to be made? What discussions have taken place about your responsibilities, desires, and capabilities in providing for their care? What are your thoughts currently about these issues? Discuss the physical, emotional, and financial concerns as a minimum.

_____
_____
_____
_____
_____
_____
_____
_____
_____
_____
_____
_____
_____
_____
_____
_____
_____
_____
_____
_____
_____
_____
_____
_____
_____
_____
_____
_____
_____
_____
_____
_____
_____
_____

5. What do you think you would need from your spouse if you were to lose a child? What do you think he or she would need? What would your other children and the family as a whole need? In what ways will you be able to or not be able to meet these needs for others? Will you be able to ask for what you need? Why or why not?

_____

_____

_____

_____

_____

_____

_____

_____

_____

_____

_____

_____

_____

_____

_____

_____

_____

_____

_____

_____

_____

_____

_____

_____

_____

_____

_____

_____

_____

_____

_____

_____

_____

_____

_____

_____

6. What would you struggle with the most if you were to lose your spouse? Who or what would be your primary sources of support?

_____
_____
_____
_____
_____
_____
_____
_____
_____
_____
_____
_____
_____
_____
_____
_____
_____
_____
_____
_____
_____
_____
_____
_____
_____
_____
_____
_____
_____
_____
_____
_____
_____
_____
_____
_____

Now that you have answered these questions, sit down with your spouse and discuss each of these questions and how you answered them. Pay particular attention to needs, feelings, and messages that are developed through the discussion.

<u>Action Plan</u>: As a couple, we have decided to make the following changes or to start doing the following things with regards to grief and loss: We will sit down and discuss our progress on this plan in 4 weeks.

(Date and time of next meeting) _____

_____
_____
_____
_____
_____
_____
_____
_____
_____
_____
_____
_____
_____
_____
_____
_____
_____
_____
_____
_____
_____
_____
_____
_____
_____
_____
_____
_____
_____
_____
_____

Author Biography

Dr. Michael Howard is a Licensed Professional Counselor, Clinical Addictions Specialist, Marriage and Family Therapist and Mental Health Counselor. He is an experienced individual, couple, family, and group therapist. His counseling specialties include couples therapy, infidelity, sexual addiction, and trauma recovery. Dr Howard is currently the Executive Director and founder of Healing Solutions Counseling Center, PLLC in Charlotte, NC.

Dr. Howard holds masters degrees in professional counseling, addiction psychology, marriage and family therapy, and discipleship ministries. He also holds a Doctor of Education (EdD) degree in counseling psychology. He is a Board Certified Professional Christian Counselor and a Certified Sex Addiction Therapist and Supervisor.

Dr. Howard is an adjunct faculty member in the graduate marriage and family therapy program at Northcentral University in Prescott Valley, Arizona where he teaches courses in marriage and family therapy, sexual addiction and infidelity, treatment of military families, and sex therapy. He has also taught undergraduate courses in psychology at Campbell University on base at Camp Lejeune, NC.

Dr. Howard has served in the United States Navy as both a nuclear-trained submarine electrician (Chief Petty Officer) for 18 years and as a Chaplain for 10 years. He is scheduled to retire in June 2012. He has served in a Marine combat battalion, at Navy Boot camp, on five different submarines and most recently as Command Chaplain of a Naval warship.

In addition to being a prominent relationship and addiction therapist, Dr. Howard has authored numerous articles for scholarly journals and has presented at National conferences and to general audiences nationwide on the topics of ethics, sexual addiction, infidelity, and building great relationships.

Dr. Howard has been married for more than 25 years to the love of his life, Lonna. They have four children (three girls and a boy), and two dogs. He enjoys jogging, working out at the gym, camping, biking, and reading.

Made in the USA
Lexington, KY
21 September 2016